KATHLEEN FOSTER
7753 LENNON RD.
CORUNNA MI 48817

Chick Moorman
and Dee Dishon

our class-room

We Can Learn Together

Personal Power Press P.O. Box 68, Portage, MI 49081

Library of Congress Cataloging in Publication Data

MOORMAN, CHICK.
 Our classroom.

 Bibliography: p.
 Includes index.
 1. Classroom management. 2. Group work in
education. 3. Students—Psychology. I. Dishon, Dee.
II. Title.
LB3013.M664 1983   371.1'02   83-3441

ISBN 0-9616046-1-1
Previously published by Prentice-Hall

ISBN 0-13-643965-9 {PBK.}

ISBN 0-13-643973-X

Printed in the United States of America.

Photographs by Chick Moorman and Dee Dishon
Illustrations by Melinda Kabel

This book is available at a special discount
when ordered in bulk quantities.
Contact the Institute for Personal Power
P.O. Box 68, Portage, MI 49081
(616) 327-2761

To teachers
who risked by opening their classrooms
and sharing themselves with us.
Teacher effort does make a difference.

contents

preface

The purpose of this book is to help teachers create a classroom environment where discipline problems are less likely to occur, and where children are less likely to activate the new three Rs—Resistance, Reluctance, and Resentment. This book is drawn from our own experiences, both as classroom teachers and as consultants who work closely with teachers over extended periods of time. This is not an attempt to sell you on the right path to becoming an effective teacher. Rather, it is an account of ideas, techniques, and strategies that have worked for us or have worked for others. It is an effort to share with you successes we have experienced and successes we have observed.

Our intention is not to create an all-inclusive text that is the final answer for anyone wishing to create an Our Classroom feeling. We intend to point the way by providing suggestions, descriptions, direction, and things to think about.

The main points of this book are potency and ownership. Students in an Our Classroom environment feel more potent, have more control over their school lives, and feel a greater sense of ownership of the environment. Therefore, they act less resistant, behave less reluctantly, and experience less resentment. In short, they cause fewer problems.

This book focuses on teacher effort and the issue of intentionality. Cooperation, interdependence, self-responsibility, and mutual respect can and do happen in classrooms. But they don't happen by accident. They happen because teachers set out to make them happen with a structured, action-oriented plan. By learning the skills necessary to create an Our Classroom feeling and purposefully putting those skills to use, teachers are more effective in preventing and handling discipline problems as well as building bridges between themselves and students.

While reading this book, you will notice how we have chosen to handle the he/she situation. We debated the issue and decided against any form of he/she, s/he, or him/herself. We chose instead to alternate between the sexes, and we hope that neither has been shortchanged.

Many portions of this book are written as if they are told from the point of view of one person. We chose not to use "I, Chick" or "I, Dee" constantly to identify whose experience was being described. We decided to use "I" or "we" without adding individual names to make the book more readable. Be assured that we believe in all the ideas, concepts, and strategies detailed in this book. Each of us has seen examples of the techniques presented. We welcome the opportunity to share them with you.

We wish to acknowledge our employers, the Region 12 Substance Abuse Prevention Education Program at the Calhoun Intermediate School District in Marshall, Michigan, and the Instructional Division at the Kalamazoo Valley Intermediate School District in Kalamazoo, Michigan, for providing us with employment that helped us grow and expand as professional educators. In addition, working for these school districts has enabled us to make contact with thousands of teachers and administrators throughout the state. We are indebted to our colleagues who have given us support, encouragement, and inspiration. Special thanks go to Pat Wilson O'Leary, who helped with the chapter on Cooperative Learning, and to Ione Condit, who helped develop and implement the Our Classroom project.

There are probably as many ways to read this book as there are people to read it. We expect that your way is as unique and special as you are. That is as it should be.

We hope, however, that you fit your special way of using this book into the norms that follow. We suggest norms because we think we know something about how this book could be read to get the maximum effect from it.

THE DOUGHNUT THEORY

The doughnut theory symbolizes a way of looking at things. Generally people either look for the doughnut or they look for the hole. People looking for the doughnut in their lives concentrate on the positive, noticing things that are useful, workable, and do-able. People looking for the hole in their lives dwell on the negative, finding reasons why something won't work or can't be done. In each case, people find what they look for.

It is possible to approach this book from either perspective. You can look for the holes, and you will find some. Or you can look for pieces of the doughnut and find some of those. We suggest that as you read this book you concentrate on what is here for you. Pay attention to what will work for you, what is useful to you, what seems do-able to you. Let the rest go by. There is something here for you. If you're looking for it, you will find it. Go for the doughnut, not the hole.

DIFFERENT RIGHT ANSWERS

There is no one best way to teach. There is no one best way to create an Our Classroom feeling. The right way for me may not be the right way for you. There are different right ways to get there for all of us.

Regardless of your style of teaching, answers are here for you. Adapt the ideas presented in this book. Change them to fit you, your grade level, and your students. Tailor them to your own best way of operating, whatever that happens to be.

What you reject as useless, someone else will use next Monday. What you choose to implement tomorrow, others may pass over quickly. You know best what's right for you. Find it, use it, and enjoy it.

PARTICIPATE

We want this to be an active book, one that you will use and reuse. It is designed to be more than read. It is designed to be used.

Use it to stimulate your thinking. Take time to reflect on the ideas presented. Don't rush it. Give yourself time to let the ideas marinate. Think through each section and determine what is meaningful for you.

Use this book to evaluate yourself and set goals. Please do the activities as they occur. You may be tempted to skip over the written exercises and visualizations. Please resist that temptation. They build throughout the book and have a cumulative effect.

Use this book as a reference. Underline, fold back pages, star items, or cut the book apart and put it in a file box.

Participate by using these strategies in your classroom. Implement some of the ideas and strategies that have meaning to you. It is not important that you implement all the activities suggested; what is important is that you implement some.

TAKE SOME RISKS

Use this book as a catalyst to practice some behaviors or techniques you might not normally use. Take some small steps out of your comfort zone. See what it's like to do something different. Watch yourself. Notice what you're like when you take risks. Pay attention to how that feels. You can always go back to your old ways if experiments don't work out. You just may surprise yourself.

LIGHTEN UP

This is a serious book. Important issues and concepts are discussed on the pages that follow. We care deeply about creating the Our Classroom feeling and respect it as an important answer for many classroom teachers. We want you to take it seriously, too.

On the other hand, we want you to enjoy this book. We want you to have fun with it. We hope you will play with this book, enjoying your participation with it.

Enjoy your successes in creating the Our Classroom feeling, and enjoy those times that aren't as successful as you hope they could be. Give yourself permission to make mistakes. Find the humor in those mistakes. Step back and laugh at yourself from time to time. Lighten up.

We had fun writing this book. We hope you have fun reading and using it as well.

PASS IT ON

Teachers sharing with teachers—that is one of the main themes throughout this book. The ideas, strategies, and techniques included here are present because teachers shared them with us. Without their willingness to talk about their frustrations, joys, successes, failures, and excitements, there would be no book.

Teachers and administrators took the time and effort to share these ideas with us. We hope you will take the time and effort to share them with others. Let us know what works for you. Call or write us at the Institute for Personal Power, PO Box 68, Portage, Mi 49081 (616-327-2761). Talk to your colleagues about what you see as useful. Write to magazines sharing your experiences. Make presentations at staff meetings. Design an in-service presentation and offer it to educators in your area. Pass it on.

Introduction

1

our classroom:
a definition

"Our Classroom" is a phrase that symbolizes strong feelings of unity and inter-relatedness within a classroom group. Togetherness, belonging, oneness, and "sense of group" are other terms that help describe the concept. As one fourth-grade class-room teacher put it, "We are a community here, and it's kind of like a second home. We call it a community of caring." It is a climate, as well as a place, where children and adults feel ownership of the shared time and space. The classroom is ours, collectively.

The Our Classroom feeling, then, takes an effort on the part of teachers to establish an environment, an attitude, and an atmosphere in which teacher and chil-dren experience unity and interrelatedness. It is a style of operating in which teacher and students feel shared control, shared responsibility, and a shared sense of worth and belonging. It is a climate of caring, a laboratory for living and growing, a time for experiencing the present. Creating the Our Classroom feeling is a process for helping students and teachers experience independent, as well as interdependent, behavior. It is an attempt to discover how we can best help ourselves and children in the time and space we have available.

For teachers, creating the Our Classroom feeling is an attitude, a mind set, a way of looking at children and the educational process that is natural, positive, and solution oriented. It is a style of behaving that gives students increasing opportunities to initiate, discover, and take responsibility for their own learning and actions. It is a method of sharing control that creates more controllers, a way of giving up responsi-

bility that increases responsible behavior, and an effort at cutting down on teaching that increases learning.

For children, the Our Classroom philosophy means opportunities to make choices, to set goals, and to have some degree of control over their own school lives. It means chances for them to participate in group problem-solving situations where they will listen, have input, and reach consensus. It means opportunities to be important, functioning members of a group and to see themselves as such. Creating the Our Classroom feeling moves beyond helping children *feel* that they have a stake in the environment. It *gives* them a stake in the environment.

To further define what an Our Classroom feeling means for teachers and children, we will examine an "our" classroom in operation. Let's take a tour of a third-grade class where Our Classroom philosophies, practices, and materials are being used.

We begin this visit in the hallway of an elementary-school building. We immediately see children's efforts on display throughout the corridor. Walls, doors, lockers, and windows are filled with stories, pictures, poems, and other miscellaneous creations. We notice that they are appropriately marked "*Our* Spring Pictures" and "Things *We* Like to Do."

The sign on the classroom door informs us of the area we are about to enter. It doesn't say "Third Grade," nor is it marked "Mr. Clabow's Room." It reads "Pink

4

Panther Territory. Welcome to Our Classroom." Thirty-one names are attached. One is the teacher's.

As we enter, we immediately notice more students' work on display. We find it stuck to walls, tacked to cardboard partitions, and hung from the ceiling. Charts, graphs, word collections, schedules, and sign-up sheets are taped to filing cabinets, the bathroom door, and other assorted showplaces.

Early arrivals busy themselves with tasks that must be performed and recorded over a number of days. Bean sprouts are measured, charted, and then watered. Two students use the extra morning minutes to add a section to a model baseball stadium they are constructing.

As we watch students arrive, we notice that each participates in the necessary morning bookkeeping chores. It is the responsibility of each child, as well as the teacher, to turn over his own tag on the attendance board. That tag indicates a person's presence. Later we watch a child record the names of those not checked in and forward that information to the office.

A clipboard, posted near the entrance, serves as the place for everyone to record her lunch status. A ditto sheet labeled "Hot Lunch/Cold Lunch/Walkers" is divided into three columns. Everyone is expected to sign under the appropriate heading.

One child spots us immediately on her entrance. It's her job to notice guests this week. Before she even gets her coat off, we're shown a volume entitled "Our Guest Book." It's explained to us that guests are encouraged to share by writing their names, addresses, and reasons for coming. We willingly consent, adding our names to the growing list of classroom visitors.

Some kids are already sitting on the carpet when the bell rings. Those who aren't set aside their current interests and join the others. We edge in to gain a closer view.

The teacher uses this time to review the day's schedule with the children. We observe on the chalkboard that the morning is divided into four sections. The agenda includes Our Hands Book, Activity Time, A.M. Evaluation, and Sharing. We listen as each is explained and questioned.

Our Hands Book becomes the first task to follow the morning meeting. The teacher initiates the activity by leading a class discussion about what hands can do. Following the discussion, the children are required to think of one thing they're "good at" with their hands, draw an outline of one hand, cut it out, and write their sentence on it. Students are expected to complete their hand task before going on to Activity Time. The individual hands will later be combined to create a class book.

We watch curiously as papers are distributed, materials located, and people begin to work. One by one the children and Mr. Clabow finish their requirements. Individually they place their contribution in the designated area and begin Activity Time.

It isn't long before we see evidence of cooperation and sharing. One child is tutoring another in basic math facts. Several students are working together to produce a group mural. The group of third graders must plan, find materials and resources, make decisions, and create a final product. Other students show real interest in the group's progress. On another day the group will officially share their efforts at a class meeting.

We notice that when one child spills a box of paper clips, four others begin to help pick them up. Help was not requested. It was simply given. Sharing seems to be important here. More evidence is the sign-up sheet on the chalkboard, which is labeled "Sharing Time" and reveals six signatures and the fact that sharing is not left to chance. In this classroom, sharing is structured as well as impromptu.

We finally realize there are no assigned seats. Tables and chairs are not *yours* and *mine*. They are *ours*. Even the teacher's desk has been turned into a community materials table. It holds the tape, tacks, pencils, paper, scissors, rulers, glue, crayons, and other common supplies. It belongs to everyone.

Two students are observed checking their own math papers against an answer key. When they finish, they record the results in their record-keeping journal and move on. A closer look at the answer key gives us a strong clue about the values being lived in this classroom. The answer key is nothing more than the teacher's edition of the math book. The words "Teacher's Edition" have been covered with masking tape and replaced with a Magic Marker message—"Our Answer Book."

Students are working individually and in groups. Topics vary. The teacher sits at a table with a reading group teaching a lesson on phonics. There is movement. There is noise. The atmosphere is relaxed and informal.

Paint is spilled. The culprits reach for paper towels and sponges. Cleanup is quick and efficient. It takes only four minutes to return the area to prespill conditions. The teacher doesn't even notice. The children have learned to be solution oriented. No blame. No punishment. Simply solutions.

We see three children leave the room and take off down the hall. They had paused at the door to sign out. This was accomplished as students listed their destination, reason for going, expected return time, and names. We are to find out later that this process was not suggested by the teacher. It was worked out in several class meetings over a period of three weeks. During those meetings the teacher and students had opportunities to share concerns, offer suggestions, and state opinions. This plan evolved from the group. It is one that everyone can live with. It is one that no one has to enforce.

Self-awareness activities are in evidence. Self-portraits occupy an entire bulletin board. Accompanying charts are headed "Ways *We* Are Alike" and "Ways *We* Are Different." "I Like Me" books created by the children are showcased on a nearby counter. Prominent wall space holds "Star of the Week," which highlights a different student each week.

The noise level of one group of children has risen steadily since Activity Time began. Although what they are doing is hidden from us by the piano, it is clear that excitement is increasing. The pace has quickened. Voices are more intense.

We are caught up in the excitement and are about to check it out when the lights go out. There is immediate quiet. All eyes turn to the light switch where two eight-year-olds stare indignantly at the remainder of the class. "We're having trouble concentrating," says one. "We can't think clearly when it's this noisy," adds the other. With that, they reset the lights and return to their work. The noise level is affected.

Students work quietly until the lights go off again ten minutes later. This time, the teacher wants attention to announce the beginning of A.M. Evaluation at the rug in five minutes. Students finish, clean up, and proceed to the rug.

Again the teacher assumes leadership, but on this occasion there is no discussion. Mr. Clabow uses this time to help the class take stock. He reports that all reading groups have met and finished their requirements. Students are asked to look at how much they have accomplished during the Activity Time, make a judgment about their efforts, and set an individual goal for the afternoon. The children have no difficulty with this task. They have done this before.

Sharing Time is next and begins with one student revealing a book he has written. Questions and discussion follow. Some students share projects. Others share feelings. We hear about books, creations, frustrations, and interests.

No one seems to be leading the sharing, yet it seems organized. People are polite. The atmosphere reminds us of a large family discussion around the dinner table. In fact, the whole of our experience on this day reminds us of a warm, positive family relationship. Acceptance, respect, trust, cooperation, and involvement—the major ingredients necessary for healthy family living—are being lived and experienced right here in "Pink Panther Territory."

The healthy family living idea is an important and convenient place to end our fantasy visit to an Our Classroom situation. We see the Our Classroom ideal as similar to an atmosphere of high-quality, family-style living. A nurturing environment is created, a safe place where individuals can determine their own degrees of risk to take while moving toward independence. The classroom, like a home, becomes a testing ground for defining relationships between people, resources, and space. It becomes a laboratory for checking out personal needs against the rights and needs of others, for finding a balance between "doing your own thing" and sharing responsibility. The Our Classroom ideal, like high-quality, family-style living, breeds caring through sharing and active involvement. It, too, is a place to belong.

The definitions earlier in this chapter, the language selected to describe what the Our Classroom concept means to teachers and children, and the imaginary trip were all designed to share with you our understandings of this concept. The analogy to family is just one more attempt to communicate what we see as Our Classroom. Call it what you will—belonging, oneness, community of caring, or sense of family—it's all the same idea. We choose to call it creating the "Our Classroom" feeling. In the chapters that follow you will learn how to put it to use in your classroom.

2

our classroom:
a rationale

A first-grade teacher is trying to conduct a reading group with six students. The rest of the class is supposed to be working on individual and group tasks around the room. Within a fifteen-minute period, the teacher is interrupted by two students who have questions on a worksheet they're completing and one other who isn't sure where to turn in her paper. On two other occasions she finds it necessary to leave the reading table to settle disturbances behind the piano. With frustration replacing patience, she returns to the reading group only to be greeted by two students who have finished their work and don't know what to do next.

"I know it can be different," she thinks with head in hands. "I know that kids can work on their own and get along better than mine do—I've seen it! Is it just this group or is it me? Where do I go from here?"

Our Classroom philosophies, skills, and materials are needed here.

Ten- and eleven-year-olds are sitting quietly at their desks doing a math assignment. When whispering occurs, the teacher looks up from her desk where she is correcting spelling tests and the noise stops. Everyone notices as a student messenger arrives with a note for the teacher. Announcing that she has to accept a phone call and that she expects everyone to be on their good behavior, the teacher puts Sara in charge of taking names. Within three minutes of the teacher's departure, there is shouting, running, laughing, and much name taking.

Returning to the chaotic scene, the teacher is baffled and angry. The children behave so well when she's there. Why can't they be responsible for themselves when she's not in charge? This teacher doesn't want to threaten or punish, but she doesn't know what else to do.

Our Classroom philosophies, skills, and materials are needed here.

The bulletin boards have been stapled in place. The thirty-six name tags are ready to go. In just a few minutes a bus will pull up to the front of the school, signaling the beginning of another school year.

For Mary Wilkins, one of eighteen Green Valley Elementary teachers, this is not a time of eager anticipation. Because of declining student enrollments, the school Mary taught at for eight years has been closed. She is now teaching a new grade level for a new principal in a different building. She is not sure what to expect.

Conversation earlier in the teachers' lounge has convinced Mary that several colleagues share her anxiety and concern. Class size has increased by 20 percent, yet money available for supplies has decreased. Staff cuts included all teacher aides and several teachers.

Mary realizes that many of her students will also be new to this school. She wants to help them learn to like one another as well as learn the basic skills appropriate for sixth graders. With thirty-six students she knows that she will need student cooperation. She knows what she wants, but isn't clear on how to make it happen.

Our Classroom philosophies, skills, and materials are needed here.

Tom is in his fourth year of teaching third grade. After attending a Friday workshop on improving social studies instruction, he has spent the weekend creating lesson plans for teaching social studies through the use of groups. He is pleased with the results and excited as he anticipates the children working together cooperatively.

On Monday morning Tom introduces the lesson, hands out materials, and puts the kids into groups. He is soon dismayed to hear protests of "I don't want to work with her!" and "Get away from me, you creep!" Something is wrong. Kids are supposed to enjoy group work more than working alone or against one another—aren't they?

By the end of forty-five minutes, Tom is beyond disappointed. He is overwhelmed and confused. Some groups are letting one person do all the work. Some haven't stopped squabbling since they began. Why can't they work together? How can he teach them the skills they so obviously need? How could he possibly tolerate the noise and confusion until they get more skilled? "Never again," vows Tom. "If the kids don't appreciate being able to work in groups, I'm not going to waste my time."

Our Classroom philosophies, skills, and materials are needed here.

The incidents described above are only a handful of the concerns and frustrations that teachers and school administrators across the country are facing. Although these particular situations are fictitious, they indicate real problems experienced by real people every day.

The nation's schools are filled with teachers helping students learn basic skills. In addition, they want students to learn how to learn and enjoy the process of learning. We have heard from them at workshops, conferences, and in their own classrooms. They have real concerns and real questions.

☆   How can I do any teaching when kids are always poking and pushing each other?

☆ Why should I spend my time making learning aids for students when they'll be wrecked within a week?

☆ How can I have children working in groups when they can't even behave themselves when they're sitting in their own seats?

☆ How can I conduct a successful reading group when it's so noisy that I can't hear myself think?

These questions are being asked by teachers who are struggling to make a difference in the lives of the children they teach. They are being asked by individuals trying to improve their own professional practice. They are being asked by people who care about children. These teachers deserve real answers.

One answer we would like more people to consider is that of creating the Our Classroom feeling. It is an answer that is currently being used successfully by individual teachers, administrators, and school staffs throughout the country. It is at work in hundreds of classrooms today.

On one hand the Our Classroom idea is preventive and features a coordinated effort to create an environment where problems are less likely to arise. At the same time, the Our Classroom answer deals with the reality of *now* and suggests a solution-oriented, problem-solving approach to the problems that do occur in spite of the preventive atmosphere.

The preventive side of the Our Classroom idea is basic. Our Classroom teachers believe that time and energy spent preventing problems saves time and energy that would have to be spent dealing with problems later.

The underlying assumptions relating to prevention are these

1. If students feel a sense of belonging, view the classroom as theirs, and perceive that they have a stake in the environment, fewer problems occur.

2. Children who come to see the classroom as "ours" are more likely to respect that environment.

3. Students who perceive the rules as "our" rules are more likely to follow them.

4. Children who begin to value their own worth, as well as respect the differences in others, are less likely to be disruptive.

5. Youngsters who begin to realize that they are an integral, functioning part of the environment are more likely to feel ownership of that environment and are less likely to abuse, destroy, or disrespect it.

Our is the key word in the Our Classroom phrase. In an effort to create a preventive atmosphere, Our Classroom practitioners continuously work at helping children see that this is indeed "our" classroom. They attempt to create a breeding ground for strong feelings of unity, group pride, and respect for others by living an active attitude of interrelatedness. On this preventive base teachers build the atmosphere needed to alleviate their expressed concerns and frustrations.

Even with an active emphasis on preventive techniques, problems occur. Children still abuse materials, mark on desks, and physically disturb each other. With a preventive base, numbers of problems and severity of problems diminish. Yet problems persist.

Our Classroom teachers accept the reality of classroom problems. They face them and deal with them straightaway, with a positive, consistent process. They proceed assuming that no concerns will arise, knowing full well that some eventually will.

When concerns do arise, Our Classroom teachers are solution oriented. They help students experience a solution-seeking process. Blame and punishment are minimized. Solutions are emphasized.

Our Classroom teachers involve children in searching for solutions as well as in choosing appropriate ones. All opinions, ideas, and suggestions are valued. The students become a functioning part of the solution rather than a spectating part of the problem.

There is no magic formula, no panacea, no cure-all. A ten-step procedure guaranteed to eliminate or prevent all classroom problems does not exist. Yet using an Our Classroom approach with emphasis on prevention and the problem-solving process will alleviate many of your concerns and frustrations.

Creating the Our Classroom feeling will provide direction, structure, and meaning to your teaching. It will give you a sensible, effective method for addressing the problems you are currently facing. It will work for you.

Belonging

Our strings tell how TALL we are

3

unity

Unity means togetherness, oneness, and team spirit. It can be defined as strong feelings of connectedness built within a classroom group. It is characterized by attachment, interrelatedness, and shared commitments. Building class unity helps students feel like they belong and helps build the Our Classroom feeling.

Unity doesn't just happen in classrooms. It doesn't occur because of luck or circumstance, or because this year you finally got a good group of kids. Unity is a feeling created by teachers who care deeply about it, set out to create it, and work continually at structuring the classroom environment to produce it and enhance it. It takes intentionality, planning, and consistent effort.

VERBALIZATION

One important step in moving from circumstance to intentionality in the development of unity is to let kids in on the secret! Verbalize the fact that unity is something you value. Don't just assume that students will figure it out. Tell them! Begin the first day of school explaining your expectations. "One of the things we're going to work on this year is how to get along as a group. You'll be learning some lessons on group pride, teamwork, cooperation, and caring for one another. It's important to me that we work as a group, and you'll see that we will improve on this as the year goes on." Make them clear, and continue to verbalize your unity expectations throughout the year.

Verbalizing your intentions is the first step toward building unity. Another is the frequent use of the words *us, we, our*. Let students hear you use those words often. Turn their use into a habit.

☆ What did you like about *our* week?
☆ What does that say about *us*?
☆ *We* can do it.

There is a significant difference between saying "Thank you for cleaning *my* board" and saying "Thank you for cleaning *our* board." Only one word has changed, but the impact is quite different.

VISUALIZATION

Help students visualize the importance you attach to the concept of group unity. Label things with *us, we, our*. Get those words up and on display.

Our Jobs	*Our* Guest Book
Songs *We* Sing	How *We* Looked in September
Stories about *Us*	Books *We* Have Read

Change the signs and charts already in your classroom to include the words *us, we, our*.

BEFORE	AFTER
Ways to Be Kind	Ways *We* Are Kind
Living Things on the Playground	Living Things *We* Found on *Our* Playground
Trips	*Our* Trips

The more *us, we, our* labels that are around, the more often students notice them. Each time they notice, they get visual proof of the importance you as the teacher attach to the concept.

STUDENTS AS THE DATA BASE

Using students as the data base is the next major strategy for building unity. To put it simply, collect data about students and then use it to design learning activities. Collect hair colors, bedtimes, favorite toothpastes, worst foods, family members, hobbies, or anything else concerning your most valuable resource—the students. Collect the data, display it, and then use it.

Student data can be put on display as charts, graphs, stories, photos, picture collages, or whatever your imagination can design. Once again, it's important to get the data up and make it visible. Use those words again—*us, we, our*—to label it.

Times *We* Go to Bed	Information about *Us*
Our Hobbies	*Our* Leisure Time

Collecting student data is valuable in itself. Displaying the data strengthens the activity and heightens the feeling of unity. Using the display to create real problems strengthens it even further.

Use student data to teach some of the content objectives you are expected to help students learn. If one of the concepts is "greater than/less than," collect some student data on family members. Then ask students to create "greater than/less than" problems based on that data. If you are expected to cover concepts concerning the clock, collect student clock data—favorite time on the weekend, bedtime, breakfast time, the time students brush their teeth—use that information to help students learn time concepts.

Using students as the data base is a technique that fits all grade levels and teaching styles. Data about family members can be collected and used in kindergarten, with sixth graders, and at all ages in between. Students can do it as a total group, in small groups, with a partner, or individually. Teachers can structure it for use in learning centers or for use by the whole class at the same time.

WAYS WE BREATHE

Have students count the number of times they breathe in one minute. Record the class results on a chart and display it. Have them find the average, mean, mode. Pick five friends and find the average.

Can you figure out how many times you breathe in an hour, week, year?

Chart and graph results.

BUTTON SORTING

Have your primary students sort buttons. Challenge them to find ten different ways to sort buttons (size, color, shape, and so on). Create a large chart with the heading "Ways We Sort Our Buttons." Compile as large a list as possible.

Use that data the next day to create new problems and challenges for the youngsters.

☆ What is your favorite way of sorting? Why?

☆ Which way is most difficult for you? Why?

☆ Which can be done the fastest?

☆ Which takes the most time?

☆ Which method of sorting creates the most piles?

SELF-MEASUREMENT

Have students make a self-portrait. Then have them measure themselves with string, cutting the string at their individual heights. Create a display using string and self-portraits labeled "Our Strings Tell How Tall WE Are!"

Here are some ways to use the student data.

1. Put the strings in order from longest to shortest.
2. Using strings, find the person who is closest to your height.
3. Make five "greater than/less than" statements using the string data.
4. Tie all the strings together. How long are they?
5. List ten things you find in the room that are shorter than your string. List ten things that are longer.
6. Guess how long your string will be at the end of the year.

THE METRIC ME

The metric idea can be used to have students do an in-depth study of themselves. Possibilities for measurement include

☆ Hair length

☆ Finger size, length, and circumference (graphing)

☆ Both hands compared

☆ Foot size on charts

☆ Arm or leg length

☆ Wrist, ankle, knee measurements

☆ Mouth opening

☆ Head, neck size

☆ Ear size

Diagram yourself. Make a "Metric Me" Book.

BEDTIMES

Collect data on typical bedtimes. You may wish to collect weekend and weekday data. Display the information in chart or graph form. Or simply list it on the chalkboard. Now use the information in a way most appropriate to your grade level.

ADD-ONS

Another strategy for building class unity is add-ons. Add-ons are projects started by the teacher, with students expected to add on their own unique contributions. One example of an add-on is a graffiti board with the caption "Happiness Is . . . . " Underneath are listed all the student and teacher reactions.

We spotted another example in a third-grade classroom. A clothes hanger was hung by a string from the ceiling. The teacher captioned the activity "Attach a Rhyme." He also attached the first word (*red*) and a picture (a red fire truck). Students then attached cards that contained rhyming words (*bed, fed, sled, head*) and pictures that represented the words. The rhyming add-on grew throughout the day and extended as far as the rhymes and children's imaginations would take it.

An add-on dealing with a math concept was created by a teacher working with children who were learning how to make change. She placed a sign on a large piece of oak tag that read "199 Ways to Make Change for $1. Sign your name after your idea." Contributions included two quarters, ten pennies, and eight nickels; eighty pennies and 2 dimes; a fifty-cent piece, four dimes, and two nickels; and eight dimes and four nickels.

Add-ons are as simple as adding a contraction to a sheet of paper or as intense as adding a personal goal as a link on a goal chain.

Add-ons take a variety of forms. Ones that we've seen include

☆ Petals on a flower
☆ Stars in the sky
☆ Balloons in a bunch
☆ Jelly beans in a jar
☆ Fish in a pond
☆ Bees in a hive
☆ Spokes in a wheel

Add-ons build unity. They give visual proof of an individual's place within the group. Students see the connectedness, the relationship implied in being an important part of a greater whole. Add-ons give continuous visual impact to the ideas that it takes all of us to make up our group and that everyone in our group is important.

Teachers structure and control the use of add-ons. Sometimes they are arranged as minimum assignments, expected from everyone. Other times they are introduced as optional, completed only by students who show an interest. Add-ons can be placed in learning centers, listed as a task for Workshop Way©, or completed by children all working together at the same time with specific instructions.

Add-ons can be short term, completed by students in fifteen minutes, placed on display for a while, and replaced within a week. "Friends Are . . . " in which class members add their notions about friendship, is an example of a short-term add-on. Other possibilities are: "Happiness Is . . . ," "I Smile When . . . ," "My Wish Is . . . ," and "I Would Rather Be . . . ."

The Longest Sandwich

The add-on holding the record for the shortest life span was created by a kindergarten teacher who was attempting to give her students a unity-building experience and at the same time to make learning digestible. She bought several long loaves of bread from a local baker. Students brought ingredients to add on—pickles, sprouts, mushrooms, mustard, horseradish, relish, onions, two brands of mayonnaise, four styles of cheese, salami, bologna, other cold meats, and lots of affection. The add-on was immediately consumed on completion.

Any add-on that takes more than a few days to complete can be considered

long term. Hooking a class rug, completing a thousand-piece puzzle, or stitching a wall hanging are some examples. In general, add-ons that take longer to complete remain in the classroom longer.

Long-term add-ons are usually functional—they serve some specific purpose. One example was created by a primary teacher who brought in an old bedsheet, cut it up into squares, and had her students draw self-portraits. She took them home, added her own, and sewed them all together. The bedsheet now hangs in the classroom as a room divider, separating the quiet reading area from other parts of the room.

Add-ons can be diagnostic. They can be used to help you get an idea of what students know about a subject before you begin a unit. For example, "Add the name of an explorer to our Explorers Chart" or "Let's make a list of 'Troublesome Spelling Words.'" Information gained from a diagnostic add-on can be used to alter the content or process of a teaching lesson, to strengthen it by fitting the lesson more closely to what children actually can and cannot do.

Add-ons can also be used for evaluation. Following a study of American Indians, feathers added to a headdress can yield valuable information on student perceptions and learning. An alert teacher can assess student understanding of transportation by perusal of a class transportation add-on.

It's even possible to give a class test with add-ons. For example, ask students to add contractions to a contraction chain. Twenty contractions and the class earns an

A, nineteen to fifteen and the class earns a B. Class tests have the added advantage of encouraging a class to work together rather than against one another, thereby reinforcing the concept of unity as well as promoting cooperation.

Not all add-ons need to be verbal. It is possible to structure add-ons so that small children and nonreaders can participate. Kindergarteners can find pictures of objects that are round and add them to a sheet of butcher paper. Preschoolers can suggest verbally the noises they heard on "Our Listening Walk" around the school.

Teacher input on add-ons is important. Your contribution to "Friends Are . . ." or "Troublesome Spelling Words" helps kids understand that we're all in this together. It's not children versus teacher, but rather children and teacher working together. So spend some time hooking the rug and coloring the class flag. Add your New Year's resolution to the goal chain. Share a bit of yourself.

Class Books

One special category of add-ons is that of bookmaking. Class books evolve from a language experience activity and result in an end product that can be placed on display in the classroom library. Everyone contributes.

Children write and illustrate their reactions to a topic such as "Friends Are for . . . ." After each individual contribution is ready, holes are punched and the pages are put together with metal rings. The result is a class book, authored and illustrated by Our Class.

According to one teacher, Judy Bloomingdale,

A feeling of togetherness occurs when we've all given our thoughts and we each have a special part in the book. It is important to keep the books available in the classroom to be shared and loved by each other throughout the year. And I'm always sure to add my page to the book. The kids love it!

A partial list of topics for class books follows

I Can	Weekends Are for
A Teacher Is	Grandpas and Grandmas
If I Weren't Me, I'd Like to be . . .	Spring (Winter, Fall, Summer) Is. . .
My Favorite Sandwich	A Time I Remember
Now That I'm in _____ Grade	As Round (Square) As . . .
I Really Like	As Soft (Hard, Fuzzy, Rough) As . . .
As Thin As	I Choose to Be Happy (Sad,
When I'm _____ Years Old, I Will . . .	Embarrassed) When . . .

| Did You Ever See | What Rhymes with *Two* |
| Our Recipe Book | (or any other word) |

Class books can be prominently displayed as part of the class library and checked out the same way children select regular library books. They can also be shared with other classes or displayed in the school library.

GROUP VALIDATION

Another category of strategies that helps build unity is what we term *group validation* techniques. These techniques confirm the existence of the group by putting groupness on display (making it visible) or by creating a class product or memory.

One important way to begin giving visibility to groupness is to create time during the day when the class comes together. It could be to sing songs, share a science experiment, or evaluate the previous day. This time is used to reinforce and celebrate togetherness and to reaffirm interdependence and interest in one another.

Attention to individualization and meeting the specific needs of each child has resulted in a move away from activities that involve the entire class. Individualization has been, in our opinion, overstressed to the point where some teachers actually feel guilty if they do a lesson with all students doing the same thing at the same time. We have seen classrooms where children never celebrate their togetherness. They simply pass one another all day long in the aisles, moving from one individualized task to another. A child may do an hour's worth of individualized reading, work at an individualized math lab, then move on to SRA individualized spelling lessons. Fortunately, recess breaks the stream of individualization, allowing for children to interact and conduct informal group activities for a while. Otherwise an entire day could go by without students having any interaction or making contact in any way.

We're not suggesting that meeting students' unique and personal needs is not important. But individualization can be overdone. We like to see a balance in classrooms, where children learn to work well alone, learn to work well with others, and learn to feel belonging and connection to a group.

Selecting a Class Name

Developing a class name can be an exciting group validation strategy. We have seen the Pink Panthers, Monsters, Spiders, Banana Splits, Barracudas, Indians, Bionic Brains, Superstars, and many others. The specific name matters far less than its use and the process of its selection.

23

The name serves as a common denominator and builds unity. Smith's Sensations carries more meaning and emotional attachment than "class," "group," or "people." "Boys and girls" doesn't hold quite the significance or excitement of Convoy Buddies. As teacher Mike Perry explained,

> Naming a class is a bit like naming a new baby. The name must be used constantly and with affection until it seems comfortable to all concerned. It didn't take long for my class to know they were the Angels, and even to begin identifying themselves as such outside our room.
>
> The Angels used their name in gym class, spelling bees, even in schoolwide chess and Ping-Pong tournaments. Mr. Perry's class transformed themselves into Perry's Angels, and I could feel a sense of unity, spirit, and identity developing that wasn't there before. I don't mean to imply that naming a class is a magic trick that will instantly foster these phenomena, but I really did see a change in the Angels from the start. By the end of the year the Angels seemed to enjoy both their name and one another even more.

Attachment to a class name, strong feelings about it, and the use of it are heightened if students are involved in the selection process. I can get some mileage out of naming my class Moorman's Marauders, but in essence it is my name, for my class, decided by me. Not much us, we, our involved there.

Consider this alternative, used by Nancy Penny, who teaches sixth graders.

> The main reason I decided to try naming the class was the togetherness thing. I knew I was getting a class that hadn't worked well together in the past. They were individuals and separate. They just weren't good at working together.
>
> I wanted to help bring them together by giving them a chance to work toward a common goal. We started by choosing a class name.
>
> I suggested that it might be a good idea for us to be called by something other than sixth grade. They recorded their suggestions on the board for three or four days. During class meetings we'd look at the suggestions.
>
> We got twenty or thirty in all. Panthers, Bears, Supremes, Super Sixes, that kind of thing. Then during one class meeting we made the decision. We had eliminated some from the list and ended up with four or five.
>
> Cuda was one that was left. I didn't recognize the word so I said, "What's Cuda?" They said, "Like Barracuda." So we wrote that up there.
>
> When it came down to the last two, it was Barracuda and Supremes. Supreme meaning sixth grade, oldest class in the building, we're super!
>
> We chose Barracuda. There were about four who didn't want Barracuda, including me. But that's what we got. So we went with it, and it became our name for the year. Eventually we all loved it. Even me.

Involving students in the process of suggestion, narrowing, consensus-seeking, and final selection takes more time than deciding by yourself. It takes a greater effort on everyone's part to reach consensus. Yet it is just that process of involvement in the choice that builds commitment and attachment to the final selection. It may take longer, but the name becomes *our* name, created by *us* for *our* classroom.

Creating Group Products

Once a class name has been selected, it can be used as a springboard for other group products to help validate groupness. Examples include a class banner, flag, song, badge, or creed.

Class banners or flags can be used as a values exercise. What do we want on our class banner that best represents us as a group? What do we want to symbolize what we believe strongly about ourselves? This can be an important values clarifying, decision-making time for individuals and the group.

Class badges or buttons can be designed and worn on special occasions. You might develop a class logo for a portion of the badge with space for each student to add a personal variation.

Taking the time to create a class creed can be valuable. How do we want to be treated here? How do we want to treat others? What do we believe, and what will we put into practice concerning our beliefs? A list of ways we want to treat and be treated can be compiled by small groups of students (five or fewer) brainstorming. Then the small-group efforts can be fit together to make one major list. With younger children this can be a total group project. The list can be fine-tuned over time through class discussions to become "Our Creed."

Students who participate in developing a creed are more likely to follow it. There is a greater chance that deeds will match a creed when it has not been imposed from above.

Making-a-Memory

Another major strategy for building unity is a series of techniques and ideas we call making-a-memory. Do something crazy, unusual, or dramatic that will stand out enough to be remembered.

What will your students remember about your classroom ten years from now? Probably not that they learned how to multiply and divide fractions. Probably not that they memorized seventeen new contractions. And probably not even that they finished *Rewards* and moved into a new reader.

Chances are they will remember the day the woman came in and painted all their faces and they shared a crazy experience called *pantomime*. Chances are they will remember the day Hester's Hermits walked to the water pond to collect samples.

Chances are they will remember the tree we planted together in the front of the school the day the hostages came home from Iran. Or maybe they'll remember that special day you organize.

Who will ever forget the day red flannel underwear flew from the top of the flagpole at a certain elementary school we recall? The drawers were hoisted to that prominent spot by the assistant superintendent of schools as his way of participating in a school event called Red Day.

Teachers and students throughout the school joined in the day by writing red stories, singing red songs, eating red finger Jell-O, drawing red pictures, writing red rhymes, creating red collages, and brainstorming a list of red words. The media center staff located thirty-three red books and displayed them on a red table. The secretary bought red ditto masters and ran off red crossword puzzles and red math problems. The lunchroom staff served red pizza buns and added red food coloring to the pears.

Red Day ended up touching the lives of all the children, the teachers, the staff, some parents, the principal, and the assistant superintendent of schools. It began as an idea to spread the concept of *red*. It ended up spreading the concepts of warmth, positive group feelings, togetherness, and unity.

Maybe Red Day is not your thing. How about one of the following?

T-Shirt Day	Banner Day
Hat Day	Bumper Sticker Day
Baseball Card Day	Swap Day
Super Sox Day	Nostalgia Day
Bottle Day	Any Color Day
Silent Day	B Day (or T Day or S Day)
Switch Day	Plant Day
Grandparent Day	Old Record Day
Stuffed Animal Day	Vegetable Day (or Fruit Day)
Pickle Day	Pride Day
Pet Day	Share Day
Hobby Day	Comic Book Day
Endangered Species Day	Senses Day
Make a New Friend Day	Clash Day
Year 2000 Day	Button/Badge Day
Hero Day	Dragon/Monster Day
Chicago White Sox Day	Necktie Day
Puppet Day	Wildlife Day
Instrument Day	Community Awareness Day

Another strategy for making a memory to build group unity is to work for a common goal. The more difficult the goal, the greater the feelings of unity once it is reached.

Projects to Help Others

A useful group validation technique is any project designed to help others. One upper-elementary teacher we know organized his class to help tutor younger students who were having trouble reading. The project gave the older students a common goal that helped produce unity, feelings of worth, and better readers.

A kindergarten class adopted a grandparent as a class project. The grandparent shared his experiences with the children, listened to them read, and took special interest in those who required extra attention.

Other class projects with a helping theme are

☆ Teach younger students to throw and catch

☆ Clean up the playground

☆ Have a welcome wagon to assist new students

☆ Visit a nursing home

☆ Plant a garden for a senior citizen

Another category of class projects that validates groupness and builds unity through a shared sense of purpose is to make something for the teacher, custodian, principal, cook, or secretary. Have students design and create an apron for you to wear during those messy papier-mâché and paint times. Let them make a paint shirt for the art teacher, a cap for the custodian, a pencil holder for the secretary, or a mailbox for the principal.

Class Trip

One third-grade class we observed worked all year long to plan, finance, and implement an all-day trip to Chicago. It wasn't easy.

At 6:45 A.M. on a spring day, a chartered bus left Kalamazoo, turned onto Interstate 94, and headed for Chicago. On board were twenty-six students, eight parent chaperones, and teacher Vickie Dove-Winfield.

By the time they returned to Kalamazoo at 10:30 P.M., the students had had a full day. They had smelled the smells of Gary, Indiana; experienced Chicago from the top of the John Hancock Building; and watched chickens hatch at the Museum of Science and Industry. They toured Johnson Publications, bought souvenirs at the Shedd Aquarium and Field Museum, and stopped at Bill Knapp's for dinner. They had twenty-six different sets of experiences that resulted in twenty-six different answers to the question "What did you like best?"

But did they learn anything? Was it worth it? How can you justify a day out of school—the effort, the expense? How do you determine the results? Where is the payoff? Will they get that much out of it?

In attempts to justify, we look for products. We look closely at the day, the experiences of the trip for our answers. And looking at the day it is clearly possible to pick out measures of success. We see such things as

☆ The first time out of Kalamazoo for some

☆ The first experience of seeing a black-owned and -operated business, for others

☆ The opportunity to choose when, where, and how to use up your spending money, for many

☆ The exposure to big, to old, to beautiful, and to different, for all

But the true value of this day cannot be judged by looking only at the products. To do so would be to miss the real guts of the project by ignoring the beauty of the process. It just might be that the real meaning, the real learning, the real "was it all worth it" took place during the weeks that preceded the trip. Let's take a closer look.

The idea for the trip occurred in January. At that time, Vickie sat down with the kids and talked it over. They discussed the site, possible excursions, and the effort, and they fantasized the fun.

Chicago was selected. It was a big city. It was close. And it had a lot of interesting places that were close together. Plus it had Johnson Publications, a black business.

Parents and administration were kept informed. Permission slips were issued and returned before other plans were made. Said Vickie, "We stressed responsibility a lot. It was my responsibility to see that the letter got home, their responsibility to see that it got back. Once in a while someone would say, 'But my mom didn't fill it out,' and I'd say, 'It's not her responsibility, it's yours.'" All permission slips were returned.

Transportation required $275. A brainstorming session was used to generate ideas for money-making projects. Students suggested bake sales, bottle collecting on Saturdays, lemonade stands for front yards, and many others. Consensus seeking narrowed the list to the four most popular and possible. They were a potato chip sale, paper drive, rummage sale, and pencil sale.

The class opened a savings account at a local bank. While touring the bank, they went through the vault, watched their money move through the coin separator, and listened to an explanation of how their interest would be earned. Deposits were made after school. Vickie took four or five children on each trip to the bank. The students kept the records, including an ongoing graph posted in their classroom, revealing how much money they had. It was kept up to date each day.

Pencils were sold each morning, potato chips at noon. Paper was collected after school, the rummage was sold on a weekend. In each case everyone participated. Responsibilities were rotated. Children made posters, read advertisements over the school PA system, counted money, kept records, distributed merchandise, and wondered whether or not they would reach the goal.

Whether the students worked alone, in groups, or as a class, they worked together. According to Vickie,

> What I appreciate is seeing the spirit that it brings into the classroom. The kids get so involved in it. There is so much working together. To me, that's what it's all about. A project like this helps build an attitude of working together by caring for something jointly. We start from day one in the school year getting that group feeling together. We're here as a family. We're here to help each other. This kind of project helps build that feeling. It gives us a reason to work together.

Vickie set a $5 limit on spending money for the trip and attached the stipulation that it had to be earned. Students created individual savings accounts at school and deposited what they earned. Parents and neighbors negotiated with children over tasks and worth. Raking leaves, collecting bottles, walking dogs, washing cars and dishes, and working in gardens are examples of efforts that added money to personal accounts.

During the trip the money was the responsibility of each child. So were the purchases. Some money got lost. So did a giant, two-foot-long ink pen, which was left on the bus, and a bag of souvenirs that was forgotten on a counter. Some lessons come hard, but maybe to learn some things you have to pay the price to experience the loss fully. The pen was later returned. The bag of souvenirs was not.

Bill Knapp's in Benton Harbor was selected as the site for dinner. Vickie got a menu and reproduced the children's section, along with drinks and desserts. Copies were sent home. Each child decided with parents what he or she would eat that night. Envelopes were returned with the selection, price, tax, tip, and total amount printed on the outside. The exact amount was sealed within. Upon arrival at the restaurant, students had simply to hand the envelope to the waiter or waitress and the ordering, paying, taxing, and tipping were all taken care of. The scheme turned out to be smooth and efficient.

Not everything connected with the trip went as smoothly. One thousand real-life pencils turned out to be a lot more than 1,000 pencils appeared to be in a catalog. And UPS went on strike just about the time the pencils were expected. Vickie adds, "There were times when our funds looked bleak. We didn't know if we were going to get there or not."

In addition to those troubles, Vickie and the class had to deal with the issue of missing money. The problem was heartbreaking, but real and had to be processed. The issue was resolved with teacher and students working it out together. In the process, the sharing of concern, dialogue, caring, and closure brought the group even closer together.

Following the trip students wrote thank-you letters. They talked about their experiences and shared feelings. They created a class book that told about their trip. And they felt satisfied with their accomplishments. Says Vickie, "Watching them watch our trip pull together really made it for me."

Going to Chicago is no easy task. It takes a lot of time, effort, and patience to pull off a project of that nature. Why would a teacher go to that much trouble for children? According to Vickie,

I've been to Chicago a thousand times, but I know there are some kids in my class who are never going to get there. It's important to me that they have the chance to do it. Not only for the experience of Chicago, but to experience all the other things that went into getting us there. Besides, I didn't do it *for* them, I did it *with* them.

Other Shared Goals

Working toward a group goal doesn't have to take four months or be as involved as Vickie's trip to Chicago. How about working toward a common goal of

☆ Collecting 1,000 bottle caps

☆ Getting a class total of 250 spelling words spelled correctly on Friday

☆ Having the lunchroom supervisors rate us "Best in the lunchroom" two days in a row

☆ Being the first class to return all the picture money

☆ Returning 100 percent of library books on library day

☆ Everyone in the class being able to count to 100

We urge you to look again at the unity-building ideas we have detailed in this chapter and to begin now to implement some of them in your classroom. Some of these ideas will fit you and your own best way of operating. Others will not. Pick some that you feel comfortable with and share them with your students. It takes momentum to build unity in a classroom group and momentum begins with the first step. Do it now!

4

rootedness

A crewelwork motto we observed in a school secretary's office said,

The only two lasting things we can give our children . . . one is roots the other is wings.

The importance of rootedness became dramatically clear to us during the TV serialization of Alex Haley's book *Roots* in 1977. "Roots" drew an audience of 130 million people and still holds the industry record for total number of viewers.

A rekindling of pride in family heritage followed the showing of "Roots." Many viewers began to research their family trees and explore the history of their own ancestors. People literally began to dig out their own roots, searching into the past, even traveling great distances to homelands never seen before.

Although the TV series had a huge impact for a variety of reasons, we believe one reason it was so popular was that it helped label and stimulate people's desire for connectedness and rootedness. Having roots is important. Having ties to history and family help people gain a sense of who they are and where they come from. It provides stability in a changing world.

A lot of forces work against rootedness in our culture. The divorce rate is one. Divorces now occur in more than one out of three marriages and are heading in the direction of one out of every two.

Parents are less often within the home, resulting in a stream of changing baby-sitters and day-care centers. When families are not stable, it is difficult for children and adults to feel rootedness.

Also, many families move often. It's even called "pulling up roots." I have moved twenty-three times in my forty years. My children have been involved in many of these moves. I believe my rate of moving is not atypical. It cannot add to feelings of permanence to be uprooted so often.

Another factor that works against feelings of rootedness is the dispersal all over the country of extended family members. When I was growing up in Chicago, all my extended family lived within a twenty-minute car ride. Both sets of grandparents, and all my aunts, uncles, and cousins lived close by. I saw them every holiday and many other times as well.

My own children have never known what it's like to live in close proximity to relatives other than immediate family. Their grandparents live in Florida, 1,500 miles away. They see them once a year—some years they don't see them at all. It's simply too far, too expensive, too much of a hassle. Distance does not help build rootedness.

Although these factors work against rootedness, you can, using strategies we're about to suggest, help your students feel some sense of permanence and rootedness within your classroom.

Rootedness as we mean it for classroom use is defined as "a strong feeling of classroom stability and permanence based on the group's historical perspective of shared time, space, and events." Rootedness can exist in classrooms. It can be felt and experienced by the students you work with.

PRESERVING HISTORY

A major technique teachers use to incorporate rootedness into the classroom experience of their children is preserving history. By preserving history we mean making and saving a permanent record of the history of the classroom.

The camera is a useful tool here. With just one roll of film it is possible to record the major activities that students engage in during the first two weeks of school, including bulletin boards, special projects, reading groups, a total class shot, classroom pets, learning centers, visitors, or any other appropriate target. Photos are then placed in albums to be kept as a constant reminder of *our* shared time and space.

Cameras aren't necessary. Children can draw pictures and write about their experiences. Although it is extremely valuable to have a photograph of Jenny holding the new reading book she worked so hard to get to, a drawing of her works just as well. Captions accompanying the photos are desirable. So are child-writtten paragraphs or stories that help explain the visual record.

Photo albums evolve slowly over time. They build throughout the year, continuously documenting the memories and experiences and revealing the changes that occur. Any significant event, special award, party, or celebration can be photographed, described, and saved.

If you take a special trip or hold an event that has special meaning, create an exclusive collection of its history. For example, if you take a field trip to the state capital, do it up right. Give the event the flavor of specialness by using a special scrapbook entitled "Our Trip to the Capital." Preserve its history by saving mementos and recollections. Examples of items to be saved include photographs or drawings, postcards, a bus ticket, and a copy of the permission slip that parents sign. Also included could be a napkin from the restaurant, copies of thank-you letters, and anything else students would be willing to share. Children can then leaf through the scrapbook at appropriate times, reliving that special memory as often as they desire.

As the class history evolves and is continuously preserved, children begin to see how they fit within the historical perspective of the classroom. They have visual proof of their own permanence within the class. They feel and see their roots.

Nostalgia Corner

Photo albums, significant event scrapbooks, and other collections of group memories are special. As such they deserve to be displayed in a place of prominence. We call it the *Nostalgia Corner*.

Nostalgia Corner is defined as

1. A special place where *our* memories of past events and highlights of the year are stored, displayed, and used
2. A place to celebrate continuously who we are and what we do
3. A technique for building rootedness

The Nostalgia Corner is truly a special place in the classroom. It is the place where history is stored. It is the place where children go to relive special times, events, and feelings. It is a place for remembering John, who has since moved to Georgia; to recall Jennifer's father, who made popcorn for us while he shared his occupation; and to enhance our belief that each of us is an important part of our shared time and space.

A variety of items are appropriate for use in the Nostalgia Corner. Consider the following:

1. *Guest Book.* Develop a guest book as one way to preserve the history of your classroom. Include spots for name, address, date, and reason for visiting. Assign it as one of the class jobs, with one child being responsible for making sure that guests sign in.

2. *Calendar.* Create a classroom calendar that reflects our time together. This is a

record of our special events and is designed to highlight experiences that have held meaning for us. Students contribute the entries. The calendar can be written, pictorial, or both. "John chipped his tooth. Our guinea pig had babies." Calendars can be fastened together as the months go by, helping children see the day-by-day account of our shared history.

3. *Nostalgia Files.* We believe that it is important to save some of each student's work, not sending it home at the end of each day and not giving it to parents during conference time. Examples of students' writing, art, penmanship, and math efforts can be stored in nostalgia files for future reference.

Children can gain valuable insights into their own growth and effort by measuring earlier products against present ones. It is difficult for children to measure growth day by day. They simply don't change that quickly. But they can perceive growth in penmanship or other areas when comparing their work in September with their work in January. The differences are then wide enough to be visible.

4. *Class Directory.* A class directory detailing names, addresses, and phone numbers can be left on display in the Nostalgia Corner. One classroom we observed added "Yellow Pages" to their directory, titled it "Our Helping Directory" and listed topics with possible helpers.

5. *Futuristics.* The Nostalgia Corner can be a place for recording and saving predictions.

☆ When will we have the first snowfall?

☆ Who will be the next two presidential nominees?

☆ How will the millage election turn out?

☆ How many seeds are in this pumpkin?

Predictions can be made far in advance. When the event or date arrives, check out the predictions. How close did you come? What are some possible reasons that you hit it so close? Or why in your opinion were you so far off?

Having futuristics as part of the Nostalgia Corner helps children sense the relationship between the past, the present, and the future. Fully enjoying each present moment, being able to recall and reflect on the past, and being able to predict and project into the future help to build rootedness.

6. *Remember When?* Collect class pictures of some of your students from years gone past. Previous teachers or the picture file in the principal's office may turn up some treasures. Showcase a bit of your students' pasts by putting two or three on display with the title, "Remember When?" Older students will enjoy looking back at their first-grade class photos, for example.

7. *When I Was/Now Statements.*

When I was _____ I couldn't _____.
              (age)
Now I'm _____ and I can _____.
            (age)

This type of activity helps students showcase their successes as well as sense how they've grown. A future piece can also be added.

And when I'm _____ I will _____.
                  (age)

8. *Time Line.* A class time line is another technique for preserving the history of your "Our Classroom." Time lines can be done quickly using small amounts of wall space or they can be worked on throughout the year, encompassing an entire wall.

They can be artistic or simply factual. They can be prominently displayed or placed in a scrapbook. They can be done by individuals or by the entire group. Whatever the style, depth, or process, time lines are a useful tool for building rootedness.

In the middle of the year have students brainstorm a list of all the special happenings that have occurred. Get consensus on which ones are really special. Then have students make a pictorial representation of each event. The pictures can then be added to a time line and placed on a wall in the classroom. From that point on, significant events are added as they occur.

A simpler version can be constructed using a clothesline. Special events are written on file cards and attached with clothespins.

9. *Experience Stories.* Write experience stories with your students. Save them. One teacher we observed lets them "hang around" for a while on coat hangers.

Each morning this teacher begins her day by meeting her first graders to create an experience story. The children dictate and she records. The words, phrases, and experiences come from the children. When the story is finished, it goes on the wall for the day while children read it, draw a picture about it, or use it as a source of words for their own stories.

When the class has finished using the story in those ways, it is added to the coat hanger rack. The story is then displayed in the Nostalgia Corner and becomes highly accessible and motivational reading material.

10. *Guinness Book of Records.* Who holds the record in your room for most basketball dribbles without a miss? Keep a book of records in your Nostalgia Corner. Then give students an opportunity once a month to break a record of their choice. Some possibilities include

☆ Wastebasket basketball (consecutive throws without a miss)
☆ Balloon bounce (keeping a balloon in the air)
☆ Hops on one foot
☆ Juggling for time

11. *Miscellaneous.* Many objects and creations are eligible for the Nostalgia Corner. The main criteria for inclusion are (1) is it something we want to save, and (2) does it help tell about us as a group or as individuals? A partial list of possibilities follows.

Awards	Class books
Class filmstrips	"All About Me" books
Add-ons	Artwork
Bound collections of class newsletters	Time lines
Charts	Programs for special events
Collections	Graphs
Souvenirs	Tape recordings
Autographs	Postcards and other correspondence
Statistics	Maps
Class diary	Milestones

The Nostalgia Corner, with the great variety of objects that can be displayed there, is a thorough and continuous way to preserve the history of your classroom. And like so many of the ideas and strategies you will encounter in this book, it doesn't just happen. Teachers create Nostalgia Corners by intention, with planning and consistent follow-through. It takes knowing what you want and wanting it badly enough to choose to put in the time and effort for planning and implementation.

Where do you stand on the issue of a Nostalgia Corner? Do you value the strategy enough to create one in your classroom? To use some of your own money to buy scrapbooks or develop photographs? To take the time and effort to create dictionaries and class books? Think it over.

Take some time now to plan your own Nostalgia Corner. Take a mental trip with your mind's eye back to your classroom. Scan it slowly, evenly. What do you see there that preserves the history? What do you have on display right now that could go into a Nostalgia Corner—newspaper clippings, special student work, a note from the principal, a copy of "Our Class Rules"?

Take some time now to get specific about a Nostalgia Corner for your room. Do you want one? Where would you put it? When will you do it? Plan your Nostalgia Corner now by reacting to the following items; you may find it helpful to write out your responses.

NOSTALGIA CORNER PLANNING GUIDE

1. List at least three reasons why you want a Nostalgia Corner in your classroom.

2. Decide on the best spot in your classroom for a Nostalgia Corner.

3. List a specific time and date you will create your Nostalgia Corner.

4. List objects you have in the classroom now that can be placed in the Nostalgia Corner.

5. List objects you will create with the class and place in the Nostalgia Corner.

6. Prepare an explanation of a Nostalgia Corner to share with your children.

ONGOING ACTIVITIES

Another major thrust of teachers concerned with building rootedness into their classrooms is to design and implement ongoing activities. An ongoing activity forces students to extend their interest in something over a period of days or even weeks; it cannot be completed in one or two sittings. One example is a papier-mache project that requires first graders to spend several days adding strips of paste-soaked paper to their creation, waiting each day for it to dry, and returning to it several times until it is completed. Another example is a clay relief map of the United States that involves an entire fourth-grade class and takes three weeks or more to finish.

Most activities we see students working on in classrooms can be completed in one sitting. By that we mean that if they work hard for ten minutes to an hour, the task can be completed. The activity is then corrected, graded, folded up, stuck in a back pocket, taken home, and never seen again. Closure occurs quickly. The children begin another task and the process repeats itself.

These short-term tasks, ditto sheets, workbook pages, and individual assignments have their value. They are useful in skill building, practice, and reinforcement. They do not, however, work to build rootedness.

Long-term, in-depth activities encourage children to take their time and experience the activity deeply. They allow time for ample exploration of materials and enjoyment of the process. And because they evolve slowly, over time, they help build rootedness.

Another advantage of ongoing activities is that they give children something to look forward to. If a child has an unfinished project that he's interested in, the project becomes motivation for that child to come to school.

An ongoing activity can be as simple as recording changes in mold for two weeks or as complicated as doing an in-depth study of the traffic flow in front of the school. It can be as messy as papier-mâché or as ordered as recording data in a notebook. It can be as basic as math and reading, or as extracurricular as woodworking and weaving. Ongoing activities can fit all grade levels and teaching styles. They can mesh with any curriculum.

Following are some examples of ongoing activities we have observed teachers using to help promote rootedness in their classrooms. As you read through them, be thinking of ways to change them to fit your grade level, your curriculum, and your level of enthusiasm.

PUDDLE WATCH

After a rain, take your students outside to study puddles. Measure the width, length, and depth of a variety of puddles. Measure periodically throughout the day and into the next. Graph the results. Devise charts. Draw pictures and diagrams. Make predictions. How long does it take various size puddles to shrink? Determine the rate of shrinkage per hour. Document changes. Keep records and display the data. (HINT: An easy way to measure is to draw chalk lines around the puddle as it recedes.)

SNOWBANK STUDY

Have each child or team adopt a snowbank and keep records of it in a Snowbank Journal over an extended period of time. Listen to the weather report on the radio as a class before you go home for the day. Then have children predict what will happen to their snowbanks based on that report. The next day children check out their predictions and write up observations. Charts, drawings, diagrams, and reports are recorded as the process is repeated again and again. Journal entries may include unanswered questions, week-long predictions, children's concerns, or anything else you desire.

PLANT STUDY

The plant study lends itself well to a total group effort. Begin with two identical plants or seeds. Plant them in separate containers of equal size in the same type of soil. Give them equal amounts of water and sunlight. Lable one plant "Mean Words" and the other "Kind Words." Children then speak to the plants over a four-week period using mean or kind words where appropriate. A journal is used to record the words. Plant growth is recorded, including height, speed of growth, number of leaves, and so on. Conclusions are drawn at the end of the study and put on display.

TREE JOURNAL

Each student is asked to pick one tree to observe. The tree can be in the school yard, on the way home, or in the neighborhood. The minimum assignment is for each student to make at least one journal entry per week. (For young children who aren't writing yet, this can be done as a total group activity with the teacher taking dictation.) Students may exceed the expectation of one entry per week if they wish. Students keep this Tree Journal for the entire school year, studying their tree week by week and noting the changes that mark the seasons. Items to place in journals include diagrams with labeled parts, samples of leaves, acorns, evidence of other life, predictions, changes, pictures, photos, color notations, and comparisons.

OUR INTEREST WALKS

Keep a class Walking Journal or a series of walking experience stories. Having a specific purpose in mind before starting a walk helps it to be more meaningful, both during and after each walk. Recording the walks in some common place helps add continuity. Possible walks include

Our Listening Walk	Take a ten-minute walk around the school. Listen for sounds. Record them when you return.
Pattern/Design Walk	Watch for repeated patterns or designs of circles, stars, dots, waves, triangles, and so on.
Sign of the Times	Watch for and record evidence that it is *this* season and no other.
Inch Walk	Hunt for treasures less than one inch long.
Miniatures	Look for very small objects rarely noticed like tiny flowers, moss caps, seeds.
Sense Hike	Collect tastes, smells, sounds, sights, and how things feel. Include both words and objects.
Miscellaneous	Color walks, vehicle walks, people watching walks, number walks, beauty hunts, helping hikes, or whatever.

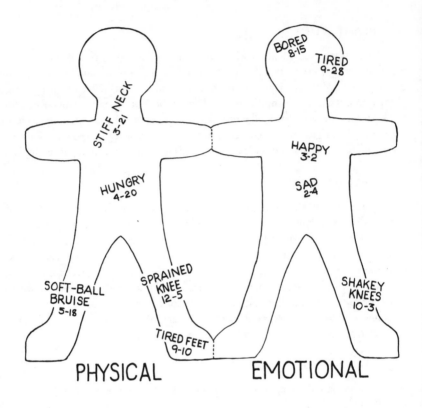

STIFF NECK 3-21
HUNGRY 4-20
SOFT-BALL BRUISE 5-18
SPRAINED KNEE 12-5
TIRED FEET 9-10

PHYSICAL

BORED 8-15
TIRED 9-28
HAPPY 3-2
SAD 2-4
SHAKEY KNEES 10-3

EMOTIONAL

HAND IN HAND

The hand-in-hand chart can be kept over a period of weeks to help children record different feelings they have had. Hand-in-hand projects are private. They are shared with others only if children decide to share them. Feet and hands are connected so they can be folded and put away in a private place with only the name showing on the outside. Privacy is critical and always respected.

EVAPORATION

Fill a clear gallon container with water. Caption it "Our Disappearing Water." Chart the progress of the evaporation until it is gone.

One variation is to have children do a similar activity using different size containers. Have them predict the date of total evaporation.

Return Quotient Exercise

Take a mental trip back to your own classroom. With your mind's eye, assume a position far above your room where you can see it all clearly. Get an overall picture of your room. Look for short-term tasks and ongoing activities. What do you see? What did children leave unfinished today that they are eager to begin work on tomorrow? What degree of balance have you created between short-term and long-term activities?

What percentage of the tasks you design for children are ongoing activities? Assign a percentage figure now. How do you feel about your return quotient? Is it too high or too low for you? Is it about where you want it?

Use this time to set some goals for yourself to help move in the direction you want to go. Now take the time to write out an "I Want" statement. Once you have completed your "I Want" statement, begin to think of activities you can do that will move you closer to achieving it. List three activities you will do to get you closer to your want.

Now go back and attach a date to each one. When will you do them? When will they be complete? Keep your activities and your dates do-able.

The final step is the most important. Do it and enjoy it!

Classroom
Management

5

managing the classroom for control

The teachers we talk to care about classroom control. Their concern with control is evident at our workshops by the questions they frequently ask.

- ☆ I just want to teach. Why do I have to spend so much time disciplining?
- ☆ How can I be in charge and still have it be "Our Classroom"?
- ☆ How can I do any teaching if kids can do whatever they want to?
- ☆ I want children to mind. Is that bad?
- ☆ If I'm the one in control, how do students learn self-control?

We hear control questions from first-year teachers. We hear them from veterans. Regular classroom teachers, special education teachers, and curriculum specialists ask questions concerning control. Educators, it seems, care about, think about, and talk about classroom control.

CLASSROOM CONTROL STYLES

We see control as a management issue. The type and amount of control that exists within a classroom at any given moment is there because the teacher created it that way through management techniques. Choices teachers make about how to manage classrooms in large part determine the degree of control they have.

We see three basic styles of classroom management in operation in the classrooms we visit—student control, teacher control, and shared control. One way to examine these styles is to fit them on a control continuum.

CLASSROOM CONTROL STYLES

Teacher Control	Shared Control	Student Control

Teacher Control

To the left of the continuum is a totally teacher-controlled classroom. Teachers on this end of the scale are strong authoritarians. They perceive the problems, make the rules, and set the punishments. They act out the policeperson role, catch the guilty, hand out punishments, and enforce the rules.

Strong teacher-controllers make all the decisions. They decide when to pass out the pencils, when children can go to the bathroom, and the level of noise appropriate for every task. They decide where students will sit, when they will talk, and who will bring treats to the Halloween party.

Teachers who employ strong teacher-control techniques have difficulty creating the Our Classroom feeling because control in their classrooms is external. Control comes from the authority and is "done to" students. The result is a "My Classroom" feeling.

With external control, children learn that someone else is responsible for their behavior. They learn to look to others for control. Students learn that someone else is in charge and that they are not responsible for themselves. One problem with external control is that when the controller leaves, so does the control. It's not uncommon for students in these classrooms to act out in the lunchroom, during recess, and when a substitute teacher is in charge.

Also, teacher-control strategies activate the command-resistance cycle. Children resent outer control and react against it. Strong teacher control encourages children to counter with reluctance, resistance, and resentment.

Student Control

On the right of the continuum is a totally student-controlled classroom. This style of control can be described as laissez-faire. In these classrooms students talk when they want, sit where they want, and work on curriculum tasks when they feel like it.

Teachers in student-controlled classrooms act as if they believe their role is to stay out of the way so children will learn. There are few rules, and those that do exist are ignored. There is little evidence of an Our Classroom environment, because in essence it is the students' classroom.

It's on days when we're in student-controlled classrooms that we like *our* jobs the best. We can leave—and usually do. Student-controlled classrooms are not enjoyable places for us to be.

We doubt seriously whether student-controlled classrooms are enjoyable places for students to be either. Are children happy when they can do whatever they desire, without limits? We doubt it.

Yes, children push the limits! Yes, they test those lines! The mistake that some teachers make is in interpreting the pushing and testing as demands for new or no limits. We believe that children are just checking out the limits, seeing if the lines are really there, seeing if we'll back up what we say.

Children want limits and they want to know exactly where they are. There is security in that—for them and for us. Too much power, too many choices, too few limits can be frightening to children. They deserve the security of well-drawn lines and the freedom to choose and make decisions within those lines.

Shared Control

Shared control is a style that helps children experience freedom and security simultaneously. It occupies the middle of the classroom control continuum.

Teachers using a shared-control style are democratic. They encourage child input in identifying problems and seeking solutions. They help students take responsibility for classroom operations and give them increasing degrees of control over their school lives. They invite individuals as well as the group to be self-responsible, in control, and potent.

"I'm not going to share control with students," some teachers tell us, "when they can't handle it. What if someone gets hurt? I'm the one the principal writes up if things go wrong. I need to be in control."

Don't misinterpret here. We are absolutely in favor of teachers being in control in classrooms. We wouldn't want it any other way. Shared control is a strategy designed for teachers who want control. It is not a way of *not having* control. Shared control is an effective way of *having* control. It often results in teachers having *more* control. More control? If a teacher has control and shares some of it, how can he or she end up with more? Doesn't sound right, does it?

With shared control students help create the rules, set the limits, and determine ways of operating. They have a voice, although not the final voice, in decisions affecting them. And because they participate actively in the creation of the environment, they feel more potent and are less likely to resist, resent, and be reluctant. The result is *more* control.

Teachers who effectively share control create more controllers. If you decide the rules then it's your role to enforce them and the students' role to resist. You can spend a lot of your time playing policeperson that way. If you and the class agree on ways you want to operate, then there are thirty-one different people enforcing the rules. Everyone becomes a policeperson. The result of more controllers is more control.

Although most teachers have a predominate control style, the teachers we see fluctuate back and forth between styles. Each style of control is appropriate at different times. If the fire alarm goes off, you're not going to hold a class caucus to decide what to do. You're going to take control and see that people move *now*! Total teacher control in that situation is appropriate and necessary.

On the other hand, when you facilitate the Valentine's Day party, you can choose a more student-controlled style of operating. Committees can be organized for entertainment, decorations, refreshments, and invitations. If one of the committees neglects its responsibility, students will experience the legitimate consequences of their actions. Insufficient refreshments can lead to valuable lessons.

Shared control is more appropriate when working with a social studies team that is writing up a group contract. Work it out together and reach consensus on appropriate goals, dates, and rewards. You agree to it and they agree to it.

Although each style of control is appropriate at times, shared control is the style most consistent with the objective of an Our Classroom feeling. It is the one that builds feelings of us, we, our. It best supports self-discipline, self-responsibility, and self-control. It is the style we will concentrate on in the four chapters that follow.

CLASSROOM MANAGEMENT THROUGH INVITATIONS

Effective classroom management begins with the act of inviting.

☆ Students will have few opportunities to act responsibly unless we frequently invite their responsibility by intentionally structuring those opportunities.

☆ Students will have few opportunities to act cooperatively unless we purposely invite that cooperation.

☆ Students will have few chances to feel potent, in control, and committed unless we frequently create those chances through the invitations we extend.

Our Classroom teachers are invitation senders. They send invitations for children to see themselves as useful, to see themselves as successful, and to notice their own importance. Our Classroom practitioners invite their students to enjoy one another, act cooperatively, and perform self-responsible behaviors. They invite children to participate in an evolving environment of mutual respect and caring.

Invitations are not always accepted. And there is no way you can *make* anyone accept an invitation that he doesn't want to accept. You can no more *make* a child act responsibly than you can *make* him learn multiplication facts. You cannot *make* him feel potent. Nor can you *make* him learn addition. In fact, you cannot *make* him learn or do anything.

Children choose learning. They decide how much they will learn. And children decide whether or not they will cooperate, be friendly, or act out. That too is their choice.

As a teacher, you have no control over whether or not your invitations are accepted. You only control whether your invitations are sent. And because sending invitations is within your control and accepting invitations is not, it makes sense to concentrate on what you have control over. Send invitations in abundance.

We invite you now to read the next four chapters. In them you will learn a style of classroom management based on invitations. You will learn how to invite students to have input, to take responsibility, and to act cooperatively. You will also learn how to manage your own mind so that you send continuous, positive invitations that have a greater chance of being accepted.

6

inviting
student input

We recently observed a group of fourth graders who were given the opportunity to express their concerns and joys about the classroom. They talked about their likes and dislikes, including what they experienced as boring, exciting, frustrating, and challenging. They shared their feelings about textbooks, specific activities, and seating arrangements.

The teacher listened and did not take things personally. He had purposefully structured this time to encourage students to share what was on their minds. He was actively seeking their input. He called it Sharing Time.

Inviting student input is one category of invitations that can be sent to children with regularity. It includes any strategy that seeks opinions, ideas, questions, evaluations, or feedback from children. Inviting student input builds student potency and commitment to decisions.

When the teacher consistently invites student response, children learn to see their input as useful, important, and part of a greater whole. They also learn to see themselves as useful, important, and part of a greater whole.

SHARING

Sharing Time

Sharing Time is one strategy that invites student input. It is not a free-for-all time when students talk about anything for as long as they wish. Sharing Time is carefully designed by teachers to accomplish specific goals.

52

Teachers who use this time generally structure it so they are in control. Sometimes they structure it to facilitate exchange of learning or accomplishments. ("Today let's share about our art projects.") Other times they structure it to increase personal understandings. ("This week during Sharing Time we'll share our hobbies.") At other times teachers structure it to allow an orderly expression of feelings. ("Let's all share one word that describes how we're feeling today and then add a sentence or two of explanation.")

One art teacher used Sharing Time to spark interest. Students came to her once a week for art activities. Her approach was to have students working in different areas of the room on a variety of projects. She valued Sharing Time and saved the last eight minutes of each period for students to share orally with one another. She believed that if students got an idea of what went on at the different areas, it would help build interest for their next visit to the art room.

Given the invitation and a nonjudgmental atmosphere, students will tell you what they think and feel about the classroom and other aspects of their experience. It is not important whether students' expressed concerns are dealt with here. What is important is that they are listened to and acknowledged. Acknowledging concerns is not the same as agreeing with them. Students don't expect you to change things just because they have concerns. Often it is enough for them just to express the frustration or concern.

Tips for Sharing Time

1. Have the person sharing share with everyone, making eye contact with several people. We have seen many instances of students looking only at the teacher as they share. One way to facilitate student sharing with one another is for you to sit within the group.

2. Structure the activity, for example,

☆ This afternoon we will be sharing journal entries.
☆ This week we will share books we've enjoyed.

3. Share something of your own. Your feelings, concerns, joys, journal entries, favorite books, and objects from home can be shared during this time.

4. Encourage listeners to ask questions or make comments about the topics others share.

☆ What are some of the things you like about Janet's hobby? I'd like to hear four or five different answers.

53

☆ What other things do you still want to know about Bob's favorite book?

☆ What do you enjoy or appreciate about Betty's art project?

Tell It to Irving

Irving (or Irvina if you prefer) is a shoebox made life-like. He serves as another delivery system for inviting student input. Students are invited to share by writing their concerns, excitements, or ordinary comments on a file card. They then give them to Irving through the slot in the top of his head.

Comments can be anonymous or signed. Irving reads all comments. He writes responses to those that are signed and leaves them in appropriate desks or mailboxes.

Our experience with suggestion boxes is that they don't last long. Usually suggestions dwindle dramatically after the first two weeks. One advantage Irving has is that his invitation includes more than suggestions. With Irving it is possible for students to share about their fun on the weekend, tell about something that happened on the playground, or say, "I like Ms. Denny. She's nice."

Journals

Journals are another delivery system that fosters written dialogue between teacher and students. Journals represent a consistent invitation that extends over several months.

Although there is no one best time to write in journals, the end of the day has worked well for teachers we've observed. The last ten minutes, after the room is cleaned up, students and teacher sit quietly and write, reflecting on the day.

Journal writing can be structured or open ended. Sometimes it's appropriate to give students a specific topic to react to

☆ I'd like to read your reactions to the situation that developed in the music room today.

☆ Please share with me your ideas on how to rearrange the classroom.

☆ Today let's focus on *pride*. Please write about something you're proud of.

On occasion it is useful to build in choices. "Please react to the assembly we had today, something you're looking forward to tomorrow, or a topic of your own choice." Other times invite students to write about whatever is on their minds.

As students write in their journals, write in yours. If you value the quiet, reflective time at the end of the day, you can model that for students by sharing how you put that time to use in your own life.

With journals, the issue of privacy is critical. Don't share students' journal entries with parents, other children, administrators, or even the counselor. Resist talking in class about comments students have written. That models your respect for journal privacy.

Give students the choice of whether or not to share each entry with you. If students elect to keep an entry private, they simply fold the page back and fasten it with a paper clip. That's the signal to you that privacy is requested. Always respect that signal and their choice.

When responding to students' journal entries, focus on content rather than mechanics. Journals are not the place to correct spelling or punctuation. We believe spelling and punctuation are important, and there are times to work hard on those skills. Journal time is *not* one of those times.

Journal time is an effort to get students writing and sharing bits of themselves. The purpose is to foster dialogue and invite a meaningful exchange between teacher and child. Nothing shuts that down faster than the red-pencil syndrome. Correct everything else if you must. But don't correct the journals!

Students in lower grades can have a modified journal experience by using a Class Journal, one that is transcribed as a joint effort by the class at the end of each day. Another means to that end is inviting fourth graders to help out by taking dictation and writing words for younger children.

We have also seen picture journals done by partial writers. Sample entry assignments are

☆ Draw a picture of your favorite part of our day

☆ Sketch out something that will help me know what you're looking forward to tomorrow

☆ Cut out three pictures from the magazines that will help tell about your day

OPINION SEEKING

Seeking the opinions of students is another technique for inviting student input. Opinion seeking means that teachers actively construct tasks that require students to share their opinions. It matters less *what* opinions are asked for and more that they *are* asked for. It matters less *what* specific opinions are shared and more that teachers simply *be there* to acknowledge them without judgment.

When you seek student opinion, you communicate to students that their ideas have value, that you appreciate and want their input, and that they possess useful opinions. Opinion-seeking tasks help children see the value in their ideas as well as in themselves.

Opinion seeking is as simple as asking, "What do you think?" or "How do you feel about that?" It is as simple as designing inferential and hypothetical questions that have multiple right answers and invite students to form opinions.

> What's *one* good reason why . . .?
>> rather than
>
> What is *the* reason why . . .?
>
> Which one of these pictures *might be* the home of a settler?
>> rather than
>
> Which is *the* correct answer?
>
> Why *might* they have . . . ?
>> rather than
>
> Why *did* they . . .?

Other hypothetical questions can be used in conjunction with your creative writing objectives.

WHAT WOULD YOU DO IF . . . ?

1. What would you do if you found a wounded bird?
2. What would you do if your teacher fainted in class?
3. What would you do if you were home alone and you burned your hand on a hot burner?

IF YOU LIVED IN A WORLD . . .

☆   If you lived in a world where there was just one color, what color would you want it to be? Why?

☆   If you lived in a world where there was only one sport, what would you want it to be? Why?

☆   If you lived in a world where you could live things over, what would you choose to live again? Why?

☆   If you lived in a world where you could change places with someone for a day, who would that be? Why?

PARAGRAPH PILES

Develop an opinion-seeking question.

Which animal do you think is most beautiful? most violent? most intelligent?

Have students write one-paragraph opinions on file cards. Paragraphs are placed in a pile. Later, two students stand in front of the class, split the pile, and read the opinions alternately. A discussion may follow.

"I URGE" TELEGRAMS

Have students choose a real person and write a telegram to that person beginning with "I urge you to. . . ." The message is to consist of fifteen or fewer words. Telegrams may be written to politicians, local officials, entertainers, sports figures, relatives, or friends. Messages reflect something students value or feel is important. Put telegrams on display. Add yours.

ADD-ON OPINION CHAINS

Suggest a topic such as the school hot lunch program or the success or failure of a recent class goal. Students add opinions to the chain by writing them out on strips of paper and linking them to the end of the chain.

IMPRESSIONS

Create an "Our Impressions" class book. Assign a new topic each week. Students share impressions concerning the new reading book, the weather, the class pet, or any other topic. Use one page for each topic with this ongoing collection. Keep it in the Nostalgia Corner.

RANK ORDER

Putting items in rank order is another way to invite students to share their opinions.

Given a small budget to spend on the litter problem in your community, how would you rank the following proposals to spend the money? Rank the proposals from wisest to least wise use of the money.

☆ Purchase litter containers
☆ Place NO LITTERING signs in strategic places
☆ Hire someone to pick up litter

INPUT ON CURRICULUM

Student input can also be invited on curriculum issues. Clearly, teachers, boards of education, and textbook companies make the major curriculum decisions. Yet students can have some influence over what they will learn. And inviting their input is highly motivational.

One way to invite student input is collecting questions. Explain to your class that a unit on American Indians, for example, is forthcoming. Tell them you are interested in what they want to learn about Indians. Ask for their questions. Tell them their questions will help you design the lessons you will be teaching.

Fill the board with Indian questions. Take all suggestions. Don't censor or make judgments. Just write them on the board as students offer them. This is not an attempt to determine the usefulness of various questions. It's simply an effort to collect information.

When you write up your lesson plans, adapt the unit so that at times it speaks to some of the students' questions. It is not important that you cover *all* the questions. What is important is that you cover *some* of the questions.

When the unit is taught, refer to the questions as often as is appropriate. Point out to students the book you've found to help answer some of their questions. Mention their input when you arrive at a point in the unit that's been strengthened as a result of the questions. Verbalize your appreciation for their input.

FLOWER TECHNIQUES

Another strategy for collecting questions is the flower technique. Use pictures or photos from an upcoming unit as the center for flowers. Arrange petals around the pictures and invite students to write their questions about the photos on the petals.

Children with limited writing skills can use a tape recorder to express the questions. Later when children find answers to their questions, they write them on the backs of the petals.

"I WANT TO LEARN" LOG

A more general way to invite student influence on curriculum is the "I Want to Learn" log. This log is stored in the Nostalgia Corner and is the official place for students to share their learning wants. They list their names, wants, and the dates recorded.

The "I Want to Learn" log is a valuable resource. It can help you

☆ Match a student to an appropriate library book
☆ Get to know your students better
☆ Assign topics of high interest for reports
☆ Group students by interest for projects
☆ Order appropriate movies and filmstrips
☆ Match an upcoming TV program to an interested child

Again, point out to students when their input is used and share your appreciation.

GOAL SETTING

Goal setting is another valuable strategy for inviting student input. Once again, shared control is accomplished through mutuality. Because many students are ineffective goal setters, have a structure so that goals are discussed and agreed upon by you and the student.

Slow learners, without direction, typically set two kinds of goals. One is so easy the student is not challenged. ("My goal is to do five math problems in two days.") The other type is so difficult that she has no real chance of accomplishing it. ("My goal is to do three pages of math in fifteen minutes.") The problem with this type of goal is that the student works hard for fifteen minutes, realizes that she won't reach her goal, and says to herself, "See, I knew I couldn't do it anyway." The tragedy is that the failure feels comfortable—it confirms and is consistent with the child's self-image of a person who "can't."

Anything a person does that is consistent with her self-image gives her that at-home, comfortable feeling. And while the child may feel comfortable for the moment, the overall view of self as "can't," "not able," "likely to fail" quickly replaces the temporary comfortableness.

Don't let slow learners set those types of goals. Work with them (mutuality) to set the type of goal high achievers typically set for themselves. High achievers set goals they have a 50/50 chance of reaching. Sometimes they make it. Sometimes they don't. But they are usually close.

Failure to reach a goal does not always indicate lack of effort or determination. It may mean we agreed on a poor goal, one that was outside the student's success level. Students on these occasions may learn as much about setting goals as they do about math. Or perhaps they will learn more about their true ability and capability in math. It is possible to learn as much from a goal *not* reached as it is from one that *is* reached.

Students consistently not achieving their goals need help. One way to assist them is to show the connection between doing activities and accomplishing a goal. Help them design a goal for themselves and list specific activities that will move them closer to completing that goal successfully.

Goal	To get 100 percent on my spelling test
Activities	Write each word fifty times
	Spell each word three times in my mind
	Get a partner and quiz each other
	Take my words home and have Dad give me a test
Goal	To be friendly to others
Activities	Smile at people
	Use people's first names
	Say "please" and "thank you"
	Ask if I can help

An additional way to help students with goal setting is to teach them to make their goals specific. Writing a specific goal enables them to judge whether or not they've reached it. A general goal is difficult to assess.

"I want to do much better in math" is a general goal. What is "much better"? How can the child tell whether or not he got there? Where is that point at which the child can pat himself on the back and say, "I did it"?

A more specific goal is "I will get scores better than 70 percent in math this week." Now that goal is measurable. The child can tell whether or not he accomplished it. You can tell whether or not he accomplished it.

Reaching a goal is self-enhancing. When children see themselves as goal setters and as people who accomplish goals, they get pictures of themselves as able. The more they add to their storehouses of positive pictures about themselves, the more likely they are to feel potent and continue their behavior.

Concern. Goal setting is fine for older kids. But what about first and second graders? They are too young to set goals.

Reply. Nonsense. Goal setting is a skill. Six-year-olds can learn this skill if you believe they can. We have seen first graders do highly sophisticated goal setting.

We observed in one first-grade room as students individually approached the chalkboard. Two ditto sheets were taped to it. One was full of addition problems. The other sheet contained subtraction problems. On a desk nearby was a kitchen timer and a goal-setting sheet.

Students using this area had several decisions to make. They had to decide if they were going to do subtraction, addition, or both. They had to decide how many rows of problems to attempt. And they had to decide the amount of time they thought it would take them.

A typical goal was "Tom—2 rows of Add, 3 minutes." Tom would step to the board, set the egg timer for three minutes and begin to work. When the timer went off, he corrected the problems, recorded his score, and repeated the whole process.

Imagine the goal-setting skills our fifth and sixth graders would have if they consistently received this type of training and experience throughout their school lives!

Goal setting can be done by individuals, partners, study groups, or the entire class. Some ideas and examples follow.

TIMES TABLE TRIOS (OR ADDITION, SUBTRACTION, OR SPELLING)

Divide the class into trios. Have each trio take a trial test. Trios then look over their scores and reach an agreement on a goal for a similar test later in the week. During the week the groups study together and help one another so each trio can reach its group goal.

OUR PUZZLE

Class jigsaw puzzles can get the entire class pulling together, building unity and team spirit. Set a class goal for completion and display it near the puzzle work area: "Our goal is to complete this puzzle by February 1!" Along with accomplishing the puzzle goal, you will find students have learned lessons in cooperating, taking turns, and developing friendships.

PHYSICAL GOALS

Students can use goals to test themselves physically. They can create goals for exercise ("I want to do twenty push-ups by the end of the year") or goals for skill building ("I want to dribble the ball fifty times without letting it get away from me").

Students can create time and distance goals ("I want to climb to the top in eight seconds" or "I want to run for a half-mile without stopping").

GOAL PROFILES

Have each student make a profile. During an individual conference with you, students set learning or behavioral goals. This is done with mutual agreement. Goals are recorded on the profile. After a designated period of time, the student also records her accomplishments.

Goal setting helps children measure their growth over time. It gives them a direction, a way to know when they've gotten there, and a delivery system for measuring their success. Goal setting helps a student see himself as someone who grows, someone who accomplishes, and someone who is capable.

This is _____

My Goals: _____
_____
_____

My Recent Accomplishments:
_____
_____
_____

Date: _____

I'D LIKE TO . . .

Create an "I'd Like to" area. Students are asked to set a goal for themselves by completing the sentence starter. Have them write it out on a file card.

☆ I'd like to learn my nines
☆ I'd like to finish my reading book
☆ I'd like to get 100 percent on a spelling test

Students then staple their goals to a bulletin board face down with only their names showing on the reverse side. When a goal is reached, the student turns his "I'd Like to" over and changes it to "I Can."

Each individual goal is private. A public display of goals inhibits some children and causes them to lower the risk they take. With total class goals, however, it is important that the goal be visible, for all to see. That creates a reminder as well as a mechanism for checking out achievement and keeping track of group accomplishments.

CONTRACTS

Contracting with students is another way to invite input. Mutuality, again, is the key word. Social studies, spelling, free reading, or extra credit contracts are all agreed on by teacher and child. That way teachers stay in control, yet students maintain a degree of influence.

The act of planning together invites students to share in the decision making. As a result of this mutually directed learning, the student has more freedom to initiate, discover, and be creative.

There is no one right way to create a contract. Commonalities in contracts do exist, and you may wish to consider some of them as you design your own version. Contracts can include

☆ Names (student and teacher)
☆ Date and grade
☆ Contract title
☆ Completion date
☆ Date for student-teacher conference
☆ Objectives
☆ Tasks to be accomplished
☆ Criteria for success
☆ Signatures (student and teacher)

Application for Extra Credit

A way to introduce students to contracting is through the use of extra credit contracts. Have them prepare contracts that include a brief description of the project, materials needed, what they want to find out, and how they will go about it. Hold a brief conference with the child to talk over the project and agree on a completion date and appropriate reward. Both teacher and student sign the contract.

LANGUAGE ACTIVITY (PRIMARY)

Name_____

Date_____

_____ 1. I will learn_____new words at the word bin.

_____ 2. I will write_____new words in a story

about_____.

_____ 3. I will tell a story about _____and use

_____new words.

Completion date:_____

_____   _____
Student Signature   Teacher Signature

Job Contracts

Help students learn about contracting through classroom jobs. Have them apply for jobs and contract to do specific tasks for a set amount of time.

```
┌─────────────────────────────────────────────────────────────────────┐
│ APPLICATION FORM                                                    │
│                                                                     │
│ I want the following job: _____   │
│                                                                     │
│ If I get it, I will: _____    │
│                                                                     │
│ This job is important to the class because: _____    │
│                                                                     │
│ _____    │
│                                                                     │
│ I would be a good person for this job because: _____    │
│                                                                     │
│ _____    │
│                                                                     │
│ _____        _____               │
│ Signature                     Date                                  │
└─────────────────────────────────────────────────────────────────────┘
```

After applications are accepted and jobs distributed, contracts are signed by student and teacher.

```
┌─────────────────────────────────────────────────────────────────────┐
│                                                                     │
│   I,_____, agree to do the following      │
│   each school day for the next two weeks.              activities   │
│                                                                     │
│   _____       │
│                                                                     │
│   _____       │
│                                                                     │
│   _____       │
│                                                                     │
│   _____      _____        _____         │
│   Student Signature   Teacher Signature     Date                    │
└─────────────────────────────────────────────────────────────────────┘
```

Earning Money

One third-grade teacher organized a field trip that involved going to another city. The class made plans to have lunch at a restaurant close to their destination. Each child was expected to earn money for the lunch and his or her own spending money.

Children were to earn that money and not accept handouts from their parents. To facilitate earning the money, this teacher devised a contract system. Children and parents signed contracts stating responsibilities, date of completion, and money earned. Negotiations were left to the parents and children to work out together.

As contracts were completed, children brought them to school. Then they were placed in "Our Book of Contracts" and added to the Nostalgia Corner.

```
┌──────────────────────────────────────────────────────────────────┐
│  MICHIGAN WITH CONTRACTS (or any state)                            │
│      I, _____, have read and thought  │
│  about the list of activities and agree that during the next four  │
│  weeks (ending _____), I will fulfill the      │
│  minimum assignment of 1, 2, and 3 plus my three choices listed    │
│  below:                                                            │
│                                                                    │
│           _____                                        │
│                                                                    │
│           _____                                        │
│                                                                    │
│           _____                                        │
│                                                                    │
│      Signed this_____day of_____, 19____.        │
│                                                                    │
│  _____        _____  │
│  Student Signature               Teacher Signature                 │
└──────────────────────────────────────────────────────────────────┘
```

In addition to academic contracts, students can construct behavior contracts that help them grow in their ability to exercise responsibility. Contracts can be written to cover a variety of skills. Some follow.

Time Budgeting. I, _____, agree to work fifteen minutes a day on math facts.

Sustained Interest. I, _____, agree to spend ten minutes on my autobiography, eight school days in a row.

Verbal Interaction. I, _____, agree to comment orally no more than five times during class meetings. I understand that I can comment at any time during a meeting, but that once my five times are used up, I will no longer comment.

Time on Task. I, _____, will only leave my seat five times a day this week. It is agreed that I can leave my seat at any time during the day as long as I have not exceeded five leavings. When I fulfill this contract, I will have unlimited seat-leaving privileges for the following week.

When introducing contracting to children, keep the time frame within their success level. A four-week contract could overwhelm beginners. A two- or three-day contract is more appropriate when starting out. Length of time can increase as children increase their ability to complete contracts successfully.

EVALUATION

Another way to invite input is to involve students in the process of evaluation. Invite them to help you evaluate products, processes, movies, assemblies, units, themselves, or anything else.

SHOW TIME

Rate that movie. Explain to students your goals in showing it. Let them help evaluate its effectiveness.

EVALUATION FORM

(Circle the one you agree with)

INTERESTING	NOT INTERESTING
THIRD-GRADE LEVEL	NOT THIRD-GRADE LEVEL
WELL-PHOTOGRAPHED	NOT WELL-PHOTOGRAPHED
USEFUL	NOT USEFUL
HUMOROUS	NOT HUMOROUS

Do you think I should show it next year?   YES   NO   NO OPINION

What did you most enjoy about this film? _____

_____

_____

What did you least enjoy about this film? _____

_____

_____

If you don't choose to create a full evaluation form, have students give a simpler rating. Any age-group can give a thumbs up or thumbs down signal. Or judge the movie with a one- to four-star rating.

Other content delivery systems that can be evaluated by children include filmstrips, learning centers, textbooks, library books, kits, games, or whatever you use to help deliver curriculum. It is not important that students evaluate everything. What is important is that they have opportunities to rate *some* things!

MY OPINION

Name _____   Date _____

What I did: _____

_____

_____

My opinion of what I did: _____

_____

_____

```
┌─────────────────────────────────────────────────────────────────┐
│                                                                   │
│   BOOK REVIEW                                                     │
│                                                                   │
│   Student's name_____    Date _____        │
│                                                                   │
│   Name of book    _____    Author  _____      │
│                                                                   │
│   One-word rating:_____                         │
│                                                                   │
│   Explanation of rating:  _____   │
│                                                                   │
│   _____ │
│                                                                   │
└─────────────────────────────────────────────────────────────────┘
```

Students are capable of evaluating their own behavior—as a group or individually. As a class they can rate their behavior at the assembly, judge how well they played together during the soccer game, or list descriptive words that tell about their lunchroom experiences. They can give themselves points as a group for respecting quiet time, assess how well they solved a class problem, or determine how well the group achieved a learning goal.

One of the major reasons for involving students in evaluation of products, processes, activities, and delivery systems is the issue of *potency*. Inviting children to evaluate is a way of increasing potency by giving them a stake in the environment. It builds their sense of ownership and their feelings of importance. Students who feel more potent are more likely to be involved, motivated, and committed.

Another issue is involved in evaluation, though it is not easily recognized at first glance—self-judgment. In our society and in our schools we teach children to look away from themselves and toward others for measures of their worth. We constantly remind students that others judge, grade, measure, and rate them, and that those others are in the best position to know. We spend little or no time helping students learn to make their own decisions, evaluations, and judgments.

We do our children a disservice when we teach them to look to others for measures of their worth. If their worth is determined by people and events outside themselves, then they spend time chasing external proof, trying to find people to mirror their goodness back to them. We want to teach children to look within for those judgments. We want to teach children to set their own standards, strive to live by them, and judge themselves accordingly. We want children to learn to trust their own assessments and use those as the foundation for their sense of personal worth.

One invitation to students in the area of self-evaluation is to have them fill out their own report cards. We watched this done in a second-grade classroom. The teacher explained to the students that parent-teacher conferences were two weeks away and that he wanted their input before meeting with parents. He dittoed off copies of the report card and asked students to rate themselves on (1) subject areas listed, and (2) social skills they had been working on. He explained further that he also would mark report cards and then make a comparison of the two. He intended to have a conference with each child before the parent-teacher conference. As he stated, "If you think you're doing great in spelling and I have you down as not doing well, we had better talk about that and find out why there is a difference. And if I think you've done well at cooperation and you think that you haven't, then we will want to talk about that, too."

Child conferences were held, differences were discussed, and understandings were reached. Students learned exactly where they stood in the eyes of this teacher. They knew what their parents would be hearing at conference time.

Contrast this with the typical parent-teacher conference. Students in this case don't know the condition of their own progress until they hear a report from their parents following the conference. Children often feel anxiety and powerlessness in that situation.

Perhaps teachers are conferring with the wrong person. We believe that an unspoken message teachers communicate to children when they confer with parents is that someone else is responsible for the child's learning. Parent-teacher conferences communicate to children, "It's your parents' job to see that you learn, not yours. It's *their* right to hear about your progress, not yours. *They* are responsible for your learning, not you."

We are not for abandoning parent-teacher conferences. We are for expanding them to include parent, teacher, and child. Take the anxiety and the indirectness out of conferences. Make the child the focal point, with the responsibility for learning and progress right where it belongs, squarely on the shoulders of the learner.

MY REPORT CARD

NAME_____ SCHOOL_____ GRADE_____

GRADING KEY: 1 = Excellent
2 = OK
3 = Need to improve

SUBJECT AREA	SOCIAL SKILLS
Reading_____	Finishing my work_____
Math_____	Sharing with others_____
Spelling_____	Respecting others' rights_____
Handwriting_____	Having fun at school_____
	Helping in class_____
	Doing neat work_____
	Following directions_____

Before students begin to evaluate their progress by filling out a report card, give them other experiences with self-evaluation. Let them judge their own handwriting, decide whether a report is messy or neat, or evaluate their behavior at the end of the day. Help children learn the skills of measuring themselves against an internal standard by asking them how they like their own artwork, what they think of their effort, or how they can strengthen a project.

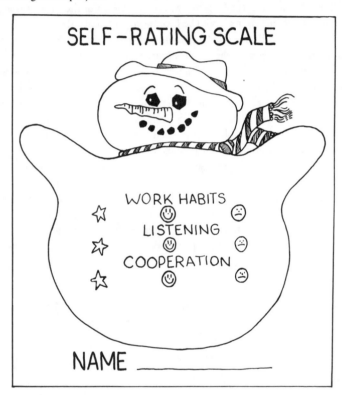

Concern. My students don't evaluate themselves accurately. Many kids turn in lousy papers and rate them as good.

Reply. Children won't automatically evaluate themselves with a high degree of accuracy. Self-evaluation is a skill and takes practice, guidance, processing, and more practice. It doesn't seem unusual to us that children who have spent a lifetime looking to others for measures of their worth will encounter problems turning that focus inward. Children who have initial trouble with accurate self-evaluation will improve with practice and processing.

One strategy for beginning self-evaluation with students is to start small. Set up a situation in which children evaluate only a portion of their behavior, product, or effort. Help them look at their work through self-judging eyes by asking them to find the best parts or the weakest parts.

> Look at your penmanship paper. Look through your rows of Rs. Circle your three best Rs. Now find some that are not your best. Underline the two that you could improve on next time.

Create short evaluation forms that invite students to look at specific pieces of their work.

RATE YOUR WRITING

Dear Teacher:
    I am turning in the following creative writing lesson:

_____

Below is what I think of this paper.

	LOW				HIGH
NEATNESS	1	2	3	4	5
HUMOR	1	2	3	4	5
INTEREST	1	2	3	4	5
PUNCTUATION	1	2	3	4	5
EFFORT	1	2	3	4	5

If I were marking this paper, I would give it a grade of_____.

_____
Signed

LOOK-AT-ME CONTINUUM

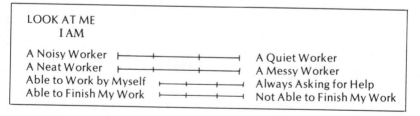

LOOK AT ME
  I AM

A Noisy Worker ⊢——+——+——⊣ A Quiet Worker
A Neat Worker ⊢——+——+——⊣ A Messy Worker
Able to Work by Myself ⊢——+——+——⊣ Always Asking for Help
Able to Finish My Work ⊢——+——+——⊣ Not Able to Finish My Work

The Look-at-Me Continuum presents students with examples of behavior. Each behavior is shown with its opposite. This type of instrument can be used in several ways. (Students who are not able to read can do these if the opposites are read orally.) Some possibilities include

Pre/Post. Students are asked to mark how they *expect* to behave during a given activity. They rate their behavior again after the activity is completed. Students then determine the item with the greatest difference between predicted and actual behavior and list possible reasons for the difference.

Real/Ideal. Students mark where they actually think they are now (*real*) on each continuum. Then they mark on each continuum where they would like to be (*ideal*). Students are then asked to keep track of things that "get in the way" or prevent them from behaving in line with their ideal. After collecting data for two weeks, students work in trios to develop strategies for improving. Goal setting follows.

TIME USE TODAY

Give each child a blank circle and these directions.

Color the circle red to represent the amount of time you feel that you used wisely today. Color the circle blue to represent the amount of time you feel that you wasted today.

THE MATH PATH

In math I have been working on:

_____

_____

_____

_____

I want help with:

_____

_____

I do my best in math: (circle one)
    almost always   sometimes   not often
Below are ways that I will do better:

_____

_____

_____

_____

Teacher-Child Collaboration

Evaluation of_____'s behavior   Date:_____

                                        Completed by:_____

1 = Outstanding   Responsibility_____
2 = High
3 = Adequate   Interest_____
4 = Acceptable
5 = Inadeqate   Relationships with other students_____

                         Relationship with teacher_____

                         Overall rating_____

Comments at teacher-child conference time:

(One copy completed by student, one copy completed by teacher)

MY EVALUATION

	Mon.		Tues.		Wed.		Thurs.		Fri.	
	Yes	No	Yes	No	Yes	No	Yes	No	Yes	No
I did my best work today										
I took care of my materials										
I did something nice for someone										
I did all my work										
I feel good about myself										
I enjoyed school today										
I respected others' work time										
I asked for help when I wanted it										

Signed _____   Date _____

Although forms, scales, and other feedback devices are useful, they are not necessary to give children self-evaluation experience. The same process can be done orally. We observed a reading support teacher working with six-year-old students who were non-readers.

> I want you to look over your papers before you hand them in. *You* decide whether or not you are proud of your papers. *Proud* means that it's some of your best work and that you feel so good about it you'd be willing to put it up on the board for everyone to see. If you're proud of yours, put a capital *P* in the corner nearest your name. If you're not proud, don't put a *P*. You think it over and decide.
>
> Now look again at your paper and check it for neatness. Look carefully at your letters. See if your letters are right between the lines or if they go outside the lines. If you think your paper is really neat, put a capital *N* in the same corner next to your name. If this is not a neat paper for you, then don't put an *N*.

We watched as these youngsters examined their papers and made decisions. Some decided to put both a *P* and an *N* on their papers. Others put only one. Some chose none. Regardless of the decisions made, each child accepted an invitation to offer input. Each completed an experience at self-evaluation.

We watched another teacher employ a similar strategy with older children. Each student had a folder of work to be shared with parents at a forthcoming conference. The papers were separated by subject matter into piles of spelling, math, and language arts. Students were asked to look over their language arts papers and put a star on the one that they felt represented their best work. Then they were instructed to put the rest of the pile in order from "best" to "not so good" work. Children rated and ranked their own efforts based on internal standards of what "best" meant to them.

Another teacher we know used a math test to invite student input through self-evaluation. After students had completed the test of thirty problems, they were asked to circle boldly two problems that they were absolutely sure were correct. They were also instructed to put a triangle around two problems that they were *not* sure about, or suspected might be wrong. When the tests were passed back the next day, this teacher led a discussion on the circled and triangled problems. Children debated such questions as

☆ What does it feel like when you know you have at least one right?

☆ What is it like for you to be unsure of an answer?

☆ How did you decide which ones to triangle?

☆ Were there any surprises when you got your paper back?

☆ If you suspect an answer is incorrect before the time is up on a test, what can you do about it?

☆ Are you more likely to miss the problems that you are sure are correct or the ones that you think might be wrong?

MUMMY BALL

Another way to give children a chance to evaluate themselves is through the game called Mummy Ball. It looks like a game of catch, but it is not. It is a game of moral judgment. It is an attempt to help students learn how to look within and judge themselves.

Mummy Ball derives its name from the concept of silence. You have to be *mum* when you play it. The ball is a Nerf Ball, soft and spongy. It breaks nothing.

The game of Mummy Ball has few rules. Those that do exist include the non-verbal aspect of the activity and a simple procedure. First, the game does not begin until everyone is quiet. Then students sit on desks (or stand) and play catch. If a child drops a throw she could have caught or makes a poor throw, she is out and must sit on the floor until the game is over.

There is no umpire, no linesperson, no referee. Students find no officials to look to for enforcement of the rules or for decisions on close plays. Our games of football, basketball, hockey, and soccer have a built-in forced reliance on officials. Each game has an external, arbitrary judge, and children learn to look away from themselves and toward others for those judgments.

In Mummy Ball, students make the decisions. The thrower sits down if he determines his throw was not catchable. The receiver eliminates herself if she feels the throw was in reach and she could have caught it. Individuals make the decisions based on their own pictures of their abilities.

There is no appeal to an external authority, no arguments before high tribunals. Each student's decision is final. The notion that each player is the best judge of her capabilities is respected. Students making value judgments on another's decision keep those judgments to themselves or they're "out" for talking.

Obviously, some players are better at practicing moral judgment than others. Students, on their own, have found a way to equalize that situation. Children making consistent and blatant errors in judgment find that they don't receive the ball often. They get the message.

In our competitive era of boundaries and statistics, Mummy Ball's simplicity and emphasis on personal decision making is refreshing. It helps students look within, learn to trust their own judgments, and rely on their decision-making abilities.

We have found that it's best if teachers don't play Mummy Ball. Students perceive teachers as judgers. If a student drops a throw and doesn't sit down, all eyes go to the teacher to see what she will do. Far better for her to ignore those situations by working on lesson plans or checking papers at her desk. If students come to the teacher to resolve an issue, they are out. If they talk, they're out. It's that simple.

Have your class play Mummy Ball. Invite students to make self-evaluations about their own abilities. Trust that students will learn valuable lessons about themselves and the issue of moral judgments. They will.

CLASS NORMS

Inviting and using student input on classroom procedures is a way to build ownership and potency. Begin by inviting students to help you set the class norms. "How do we want to be treated here?" is the question.

Early in the year have students individually write out five responses to the question, "How do I want to be treated?" (Younger children can do this exercise orally.) Students then select a partner and exchange their responses verbally. Each pair is instructed to talk over the responses and create one new list with five agreed-upon responses to the same question.

Each pair then joins another pair and the process is repeated. When the foursomes complete their lists, they write them on chart paper, sign them, and display them. Each group is then asked to give a report, describing the intent of each item. This is your opportunity to help students see that words are interpreted differently by different people. "We want to be treated fairly" is one students often suggest. So what is "fair"? What does that mean? What one person thinks is fair another person feels is unfair. Challenge the group to explain what they mean by "fair." Emphasis here is on understanding the real intent of each item rather than on agreement.

As the discussion proceeds, continually work at making the norms specific. If "fair" means that everyone gets an equal chance to do special things for the teacher, then write that on the suggested norms instead of the word *fair*. Eliminate words that are open to interpretation.

"We want to be treated with respect." What is "respect"? What does it look like? How do you know when you're getting it or not getting it? What are "polite," "courteous," "cooperative," "friendly," "nice," and "good"? Talk it out! Find out specifically how your children want to be treated.

Once you have agreement on the meaning of the items listed, begin the process of getting total group consensus on which ones you and and the class want as norms. Invite students to suggest which items they are willing to live by. Encourage dialogue.

Creating class norms may take several days, or it may occur more quickly. Don't hurry the process. Going through it stimulates thinking, builds commitment and ownership, and leaves an expectancy in students' minds that what they have to say in this class is important and is going to be valued and used.

When the norms are complete, post them in an area visible to all. Explain that they can be altered by addition, deletion, or modification at any time. Set a date to check back with students and see if the norms are functioning. Modify if necessary at that time.

Setting up norms is a preventive strategy, one that helps create a climate where discipline problems are less likely to occur. Yet even with a successful preventive climate, some problems still arise. For students who consistently ignore norms, or for special problem situations that occur, a problem-solving process is needed.

THE PROBLEM-SOLVING PROCESS

The problem-solving process is a tool to be used when prevention doesn't prevent. It is exactly what the words suggest—a process for solving problems. This process can be used one on one between teacher and child. It can be used with a group of children who have a similar problem. Or it can be used with the entire class during a class meeting. Regardless of when it's used, the components remain constant.

Step 1
Have a Need

It is important to have some reason to come together. This can be initiated by a student or the teacher. It could be about a playground-related problem that a child is concerned with, or a classroom management difficulty the teacher has noticed. Whichever, one person must have a need.

Step 2
Check Perceptions

This step in the process is designed to share perceptions. Whoever initiates the meeting shares his perceptions first. If it's you, tell the students what you saw and how often you saw it. Share your concerns with them about the situation and your reasons for being concerned. During this phase students listen without speaking.

When you're finished sharing your perceptions, seek theirs. Now it's your turn to listen. Occasionally ask clarifying questions. "What does it look like to you? What does it feel like? How do you see it differently?" Listen until they have said all they want to say about their experiences with this problem. When you achieve general agreement on perceptions, move on to the next step.

Step 3
State the Problem

What is the problem exactly? It is important to write out a problem statement, put it on chart paper, and make it visible. It is easier to discuss wording if it's displayed where all can see it. Having the problem written down provides a focus for the discussion to follow. It keeps the purpose of your efforts visible, and if the conversation begins to drift, you can point to the written problem statement and remind students of the problem that you're working on now.

Step 4
List Solutions

This is the brainstorming step during which students are asked to list ways we can solve our problems. Collect as many alternatives as possible. List every solution suggested without comment. Take the time to write out all the ideas, regardless of grade level or reading abilities of students. It helps students feel potent and valuable to see their ideas written down, even if they aren't able to read them yet.

Don't take time to talk about suggestions during brainstorming. Evaluating ideas is limiting. It shuts off the free flow of suggestions. The strategy here is to generate ideas, not rate and classify them. Don't stop with the first few ideas that seem reasonable to you. Continue to collect ideas until the idea producers have exhausted their supply.

It is helpful during this phase of the process to remind students that solutions are desired, not punishments. You are not looking for ways to punish, you're looking for ways to see that the problem doesn't happen again.

Step 5
Reach Consensus

This step is designed to answer the question "How are we going to solve this problem?" Ask students to confine their remarks to the solutions they think have the best chance of working. Keep the focus positive. Some ideas are obviously more useful than others. Concentrate on those. If you don't tear down less practical solutions, students responsible for them will be more likely to suggest ideas in the future.

Choose a solution to *do* something rather than one to *stop* doing something. It is easier to create a condition you want than to eliminate a condition you don't want. Examples are

> Borrow a pencil during reading time
> > rather than
>
> Don't sharpen pencils during reading time
>
> Wait for the person talking to finish her sentence before you talk
> > rather than
>
> Don't interrupt

Occasionally a third alternative emerges. Suggestions like "One person gets a drink at a time" and "Line up for drinks by the closet" can be combined to create a solution of "Line up four feet away from the person who is drinking." The third alternative phenomenon makes it easier to reach consensus because more people own the solution.

Step 6
Use Role Playing

Role playing is an optional step. It serves two purposes. First, it gives you a chance to field-test the solution. If you notice problems when you role-play the proposed solution, you have a chance to make alterations before implementing it.

Second, role playing plants a positive picture in the students' minds. By seeing a successful run-through of their solution, students have an image of what success looks like. And because they have a positive picture in their minds, they know what to look for and are more likely to recognize it when they see it.

Step 7
Make a Commitment

Once consensus is reached, it is important to seal the deal. Have everyone raise hands, put thumbs up, or sign off on a contract. This symbolic gesture is an act of closure that signifies you all agree or are all willing to go along for the good of the group.

Step 8
Check It Out

This step is critical. When you reach consensus, set up a "check it out" time. Allow enough time to give the proposed solution a real test, but not so much time that children lose interest in the process. Three to five days works well. Write the "check it out" time on chart paper with the problem and the proposed solution. Post that in plain sight.

Problem	Dangerous behavior around the drinking fountain.
Solution	We will leave four feet between the person drinking and the next person in line.
Check it out time	One week from today—Thursday, October 15, 1:00 P.M.

Checking back on solutions is important for several reasons. First, if the solution is working, you can use that time to congratulate yourselves and to celebrate your problem-solving ability. This is the time to rejoice in success and remind yourselves, "We did it!"

Second, if the solution is not working, you can go back to the drawing board. Continue the search for a solution by repeating the process (Step 9) if necessary.

A third reason for a "check it out" time is to communicate to children that evaluating their own solution is part of the process. They learn that when they implement a solution, they will be asked later how it is working. They realize there will be an accounting, and they know they will be involved in taking stock.

Step 9
Repeat the Process

Occasionally a solution proves ineffective and it becomes necessary to repeat the process. By repeating the process, children learn persistence; they see that problems are not always solved with the first solution. They also learn to see a solution that didn't work as a solution that didn't work, not as a failure.

Concern. What if the students come up with an unworkable solution?

Reply. In the problem-solving process, specific outcomes are not important. It doesn't really matter which solution is selected. What is crucial is that children learn the process. The skill of learning to make decisions is more important than the decision itself.

Have faith in the process. Act as if it will work everytime. On those occasions when it doesn't produce a workable solution, return to the process and go through it again. Believe that students will learn as much from an unsuccessful selection as they will from a successful one. They may learn

☆ Mistakes are not a catastrophe

☆ Seeking solutions is a process and a life-style

☆ Problems aren't always solved on the first try

☆ Few solutions are permanent; life is a process of adjustment, readjustment, and fine-tuning

Concern. How can I justify taking the time to do this when I'm expected to teach basic skills?

Reply. Involving students in the problem-solving process will save you time in the long run. When students help define problems, search for solutions, and reach consensus they are more likely to follow those solutions. When students are committed to the solutions and implement them, you spend less time enforcing. Time not spent enforcing solutions can be spent teaching, and time spent teaching can be spent on the basics.

Actually, the problem-solving process *is* basic. The more we teach a child to be solution oriented and confident in personal problem solving, the better we have prepared her for a life of challenge, risk, and self-responsibility. When children learn the process of problem-solving, they have learned a process that they can use again and again to enhance the quality of their living and learning. What could be more basic?

The rationale for taking the time, effort, and energy to involve students in the problem-solving process is varied and extensive. The next few paragraphs contain the essence of our beliefs about why the process is basic.

Solution Seeking

The problem-solving process helps create for students and teachers a solution-seeking mind set. Time and effort is focused on finding solutions. Blaming and punishing for something that happened in the past are *not* useful. Finding a solution so that there is improvement in the future *is* useful. Our Classroom teachers invite students to perceive themselves as part of the solution rather than drawing attention to how they are part of the problem.

Common Opponent

Students and teachers who repeatedly use the problem-solving process learn to see the problem as the opponent, not each other. They realize the opponent can be beaten, the problem solved, by working together. The process puts teachers and students on the same side.

Cohesion

This process builds group cohesiveness and feelings of belonging. As students improve their ability to work together, they experience interrelatedness and feel more connected. Notions of us, we, our are strengthened.

The more a class works together to solve mutual problems, the more clearly they see themselves as not only a unit, but a problem-solving unit. What a useful, healthy way for a class to picture itself.

Ownership

Students do not always "own" their problems. They try to evade by

☆ Putting it on someone else ("He made me do it!")
☆ Lying their way out of a situation ("I didn't do it!")
☆ Sweeping it under a rug and ignoring the problem ("What problem?")
☆ Giving up ("I can't do it!")
☆ Depending on others ("It's your job to solve problems. Not mine.")

Repeated use of the problem-solving process helps students face problems, accept ownership, and generate solutions. They learn to see themselves as functioning solution seekers rather than disinterested spectators.

Self-Responsibility

The problem-solving process fosters self-responsibility and self-discipline. Children learn to look inward for solutions and to trust their own judgments and problem-solving abilities. They learn to be responsible for their collective and individual selves by facing problems and solving them rather than letting others solve problems for them. They learn to rely on themselves and one another.

The essence of self-responsibility and self-discipline is making a plan and following through on it. When students decide to do something, than act in accordance with that decision, they experience self-control. They feel their power and their potency.

Reality Basis

Our final rationale for using this process is that it is deeply related to reality. It brings real situations to school and touches the real lives of our students. A variety of real issues surface during the school year. Problems like the ones below don't need to be dreamed up. They simply occur and provide an excellent opportunity for problem-solving practice.

☆ Finding alternatives to saying "Shhh" when you want your neighbor to be quiet

☆ Deciding how to decorate our class tepee

☆ Creating ways to deal with people who won't take their "outs" during dodge ball

☆ Figuring out how to control mud being tracked in after recess

These situations touch our living and test our ability to cooperate and live together in mutual respect. They provide *real* practice finding *real* solutions to *real* problems.

What real-life problems occur in your classroom? What issues recur so often that you'd like to eliminate them forever? What problems are begging to be solved? What irritations, frustrations, or concerns would you be willing to submit to the process?

Take some time now to set some goals for yourself.

PROBLEM-SOLVING PROCESS GOAL SETTING

1. List five regularly occurring problems that you would be willing to submit to the problem-solving process.
2. Star the one you feel is most important.
3. Place an X by the one that is least emotionally charged, one you could do with students without generating strong emotions.
4. Set a date and time to hold your first class meeting.
5. I expect the problem-solving process to _____.

During the problem-solving process, lead and facilitate the discussion. You are in charge here, structuring the process to ensure an orderly flow that produces an end product.

A few rules are necessary. A procedure can be set up to give and take the floor without everyone talking at once. Hand raising or some other similar signal is appropriate. We have seen teachers use a stuffed animal or bean bag to indicate who has the floor. Only the child holding the bean bag speaks. When the person is finished he passes the bean bag on.

Listen actively. Give lots of wait time and eye contact. Use body language that lets the speaker know you're there with her. Lean slightly toward the speaker as she speaks. Be nonjudgmental. Nothing shuts students off more quickly than someone judging what they are saying. Class discussions are not an appropriate time to correct grammar. Just be there, hear, and record.

It's also your role to keep students focused on the task. Occasionally they require a reminder of their responsibility to define a problem, find solutions, and develop a plan. Effective faciliation helps students move continuously toward the goal of solving "our" problem.

Whether working with the whole class or a small group of youngsters, sitting in a circle is important. The face-to-face aspect of a circle heightens eye contact, increases intimacy, and communicates equality.

Create a special place to solve problems. If you go to the trouble of pushing the desks back so that chairs can be placed in a tight circle, or if you take the time to go down to the library to sit on the carpeted floor, the message to students is "This activity must be important."

A special place for meetings of smaller groups of children is important also. One teacher used the class tepee for holding powwows when necessary. Another used an oval throw rug. She placed a masking tape X on each end of it. Students were instructed to sit on the Xs, facing each other, and work things out.

When you begin the problem-solving process, don't start with your most severe problem. Practice on some light topics where strong emotion is not activated. Teach students the process while planning the Valentine's party or deciding how to select a child of the week. Then when students are emotionally charged following a fight or heated disagreement, they will have the structure to fall back on and can concentrate their efforts on the situation to be solved rather than on learning the process.

Summary

The problem-solving process, self-evaluation techniques, goal setting, and opinion-seeking tasks are all ways to invite student input. None of these done in isolation will result in increased classroom control. It requires a consistent effort at sharing control by using these strategies to help students feel potent and responsible. It takes a structured, ongoing plan of inviting student input to move you closer to being in control through creating an Our Classroom feeling.

PLANNING GUIDE

How do you measure your success at inviting student input? Where is your comfort zone in terms of seeking student input and using it? How much is enough and how much is not enough for you? To measure your success, rate yourself using the self-assessment items that follow.

REAL

0	1	2	3	4	5	6	7	8	9	10
Low										High

IDEAL

0	1	2	3	4	5	6	7	8	9	10
Low										High

1. To what extent do you see yourself as an inviter of student input? Place an *X* on the *real* graph near the number you feel best represents your *current* level of inviting student input. This is how you see yourself now.

   On the *ideal* graph, place an *X* near a number you feel best represents your *desired* level of inviting student input. This indicates your ideal level of implementation.

   If your *real* score is lower than your *ideal* score, proceed by writing your responses to the following statements. If your *real* score is higher, or the same as your *ideal* score, skip over these next four steps.

2. I now invite student input approximately _____ times a week. I would like to change that to _____ times a week. Something I will do to help me make the change is (be specific):

3. Two things I can do to help see that the above happens are:

4. I can get ideas for inviting student input from (a person or place):
   The person I can best talk to about these activities is:
   Other people in my building on whom I can count for support include:

5. An important phrase that I like to keep in mind is:
   A quotation from this chapter that has meaning to me is:
   I like it when I:

Read this entire exercise through before you begin.

Sit back and relax. Center yourself in the chair. Get comfortable. Let your arms and legs go limp. Close your eyes. Concentrate on your breathing. Take long, slow, deep breaths. On each in-breath take in relaxation. On each out-breath exhale tension. In with relaxation, out with tension. In, relax. Out, release tension. Tell yourself to relax more as you breathe deeper. When you are relaxed, use your mind's eye to see yourself facilitating a class meeting. Notice the students sitting in a circle hunched forward, intent on listening and contributing. See their interest and involvement. Notice your behavior as you skillfully guide the creation of a problem statement and list possible solutions.

Notice your success as students respond with consensus and share a common commitment. Watch closely as their feelings of power grow. See it on their faces. See it on your face too.

Concentrate on your feelings of success. Pay attention to how good it feels to run effective class meetings. Pat yourself on the back. When you finish enjoying the positive pictures, slowly open your eyes and return.

See Chapter 10 for ways you can use positive picturing for your students as well as yourself.

If you want to invite student input to help build the Our Classroom feeling, implementation is the key. Increased awareness of the benefits of inviting student input is not enough. Classroom management through shared control takes action—your action. Act now by inviting your students to participate in an atmosphere of mutual caring by implementing the strategies that have meaning to you. Do it now.

7

inviting student responsibility

I won't give these kids any responsibility until they show me they can handle it.

My students expect to be given responsibility, yet they don't act like it.

When my children learn to be responsible, then I'll give them some responsibility.

Statements like those above have been shared with us by teachers we work with, by people we meet at conferences, and by participants who attend our workshops. We hear the comments often enough to lead us to believe that they do not reflect isolated incidents.

The words aren't always the same, but the theme remains constant: "If children would just act more responsibly, then I'd give them more responsibility."

The words that I used as a fifth-grade teacher were these: "OK, that's it! Break up your groups. Get back in your seats. No more responsibility for you until you can show me that you're responsible!" When I used those words with students they sounded good to me. I believed that I was modeling sharing my feelings and proudly displayed my anger. I congratulated myself for my honesty and my display of humanness.

Today I've come to a different interpretation of those words. I now believe they don't make sense. The words seem logical enough at first glance. Yet the logic doesn't hold up when applied to other subject areas, such as math. Can you imagine a teacher saying, "OK, That's it! No more math for this class until you show me you can do math"? Would a teacher take math away from students because they made mistakes in math? Of course not. She wouldn't do that because she recognizes that the way students learn math is by making mistakes and learning from those mistakes. Responsibility is no different from math in that regard. Students learn by making mistakes, having those mistakes pointed out to them, and then correcting those mistakes.

Responsibility can be viewed in the same light as math or any subject area. With math, as with responsibility, children learn from making mistakes. The mistakes create possibilities for learning. If children don't make mistakes they aren't learning anything. They've already learned it.

Responsibility is like any other issue in the teaching-learning process. It cannot be taught. It can only be learned. And responsibility is best learned by students who receive repeated invitations from teachers to *be* responsible and *see* themselves as responsible.

Teachers cannot *make* students act responsibly. Children are the ones who decide whether or not they will act responsibly. They are in control of their own behavior. Because students always make the final choice of how to act, a teacher's best chance of influencing that act is through issuing invitations—invitations to act responsibly.

We believe in sending a continuous variety of invitations to students to act responsibly because

☆ The more invitations sent, the more invitations accepted

☆ The more invitations accepted, the more opportunities students have to see themselves as self-responsible

☆ The more opportunities students have to see themselves as self-responsible, the more likely they will be to choose to embrace that view of themselves

☆ The more students see themselves as self-responsible, the more they will behave in accordance with that view

☆ The more often students act in self-responsible ways, the more they will see themselves as self-responsible

We think that children act out of their beliefs. If they believe they are slow learners, they act like slow learners. If they believe they are troublemakers, they act like troublemakers. If students are continuously proving their beliefs to themselves (and we think they are), then we want them to believe in their own self-responsibility.

STEPS TO
SELF-RESPONSIBILITY

Helping students see themselves as responsible is no easy task. For some students it is a year-long process, with small steps reason enough for celebration. For others it happens more quickly and the results are more visible. The process of helping children learn to see themselves as self-responsible contains six steps. In each case the process begins with invitations.

Step 1. Set up a situation where students have a chance to be responsible. This invitation can be an opportunity to check their own work, help one another, take responsibility for room cleanup, or any of the other ideas in this chapter.

Step 2. Act as if everyone in the room will accept the invitation and act responsibly. Remember, you get what you expect.

Step 3. Observe. Pay attention to what students do with your invitation. Collect data. Notice who accepts the invitation and who doesn't.

Step 4. Intervene when necessary. Some students will show you that they aren't accepting the invitation or they don't have the skills necessary to do so. This is the time to give guidance and direction. Treat the mistakes in responsibility the same way you treat mistakes in math. Help your students learn from their mistakes. Remember, sometimes students have to do something poorly before they learn to do it well.

Occasionally during this step it will be necessary to use the problem-solving process (Chapter 6) with an individual or small group of students. That process is useful in giving students input into learning how to act responsibly.

Step 5. Issue more invitations to students to act responsibly. Each new invitation is a chance for students to show you they've learned and to show themselves that they are now able.

Step 6. Repeat the process. And repeat it as many times as necessary. Be patient with your students and their reactions to your invitations. Some students don't accept invitations right away. Some require more guidance and direction than others.

The rest of this chapter discusses invitations. In it you will learn how to invite by creating situations in which children learn to (1) see themselves and one another as capable, (2) think of themselves and others as able, and (3) come to believe in themselves as self-responsible.

MAKING YOURSELF DISPENSABLE

An effective strategy for inviting student responsibility is a way of thinking and operating termed "making yourself dispensable." Think about it. It could be that your main role as a teacher is to make yourself dispensable.

Everything you do as a teacher to make yourself dispensable helps someone become less dependent. And everything you do that makes you indispensable to that classroom makes other people more dependent—dependent on you.

We have never talked to any teacher anywhere who ever said, "I'm trying to create dependent learners." Teachers don't talk that way. They say, "I want to help students become more independent. I want them to take ever-increasing control over their school lives." If that is your desire, then it is appropriate to use the ideas in this chapter to make yourself dispensable.

Class Jobs

One way to begin making yourself dispensable is to have students assume the class jobs. Cleaning the sink, erasing the boards, emptying the pencil sharpener, or taking attendance are all jobs any child can experience. When students have teachers who do all the cleanup, take care of the class pet, and handle most responsibilities themselves, those students miss opportunities to learn lessons in responsibility. To learn responsibility, students have to have opportunities to practice and exercise it. Classroom jobs are one place where you may begin.

Common Supplies

Another simple way to make yourself dispensable is to get the materials out where children can get at them. If you're making twelve trips a day to the top shelf of the teacher's closet to get supplies for students, then you're indispensable to that environment. Chances are you need the children more than they need you.

One teacher created a common materials area by spreading butcher paper over a table and taping it underneath. Then she laid all the materials out on the table, traced around them, and put the objects back. When a student took the scissors, the outline and the word *scissors* were left as a reminder of where they were to be returned.

Other Experts

Another technique for sharing control through making yourself dispensable is to create other experts and put them to use. If you teach kindergarten, you're not the only shoe-tying expert in the class. If you teach second grade, you're not the only one there who knows how to make change. Fifth-grade teachers don't have exclusive ability to add and subtract fractions. Whatever your grade level, whatever content you want to deliver, there are other experts sitting out there in your class. Identify them. Put them to use.

Concern. That's not fair to the gifted students. They worked hard to finish their assignments. They should be able to use their time to learn additional skills. Why should they have to help slower students learn?

Reply. Students who teach material to others strengthen their own mastery and retention of that material. Amount of material remembered and length of time it is remembered increase when students teach that material to others. Structuring the environment to use student experts helps the bright students increase retention of material, helps the slower students learn the material, and helps you make yourself dispensable. It also helps create an Our Classroom feeling.

We see classrooms where twelve children sit with their hands in the air waiting for help from the teacher. The teacher moves from child to child as rapidly as he can assisting those who are stuck. In the meantime, several students sit and wait. Not only does this waste student time that could be spent on the task, it also communicates to children, "The teacher is the only person who can help here!"

Let students know there are many sources of help in your classroom. Design a helping station—some person or place where students can help one another. Let the "math expert" wear a special "math expert hat." Students with questions on math problems must first seek out the person wearing the "math hat." If they don't get satisfaction there, then they go on to you.

One teacher uses other experts when new materials are introduced. We observed on the day she placed Cuisenaire rods on a table along with a ditto sheet full of activities. The first few students who used that area experienced trouble figuring out what to do and how to do it, so she spent some time working with them. When they finished at that area, the teacher posted a sheet of paper containing their names with the caption "People Who Have Worked Here." Then when someone got stuck, the student checked the "expert" list and chose a classmate to consult.

Create a helping area to promote the use of other experts. Set up a special table where a few math experts work on their own lessons. Students requiring help choose one person at the helping area and ask for assistance. A helping area helps students with subject matter, but it also helps them learn how to ask for, receive, and appreciate help.

One problem with using other experts is that students who are experts in math or reading aren't necessarily experts in helping. Some students believe helping means doing the work for the other person. Children can learn the difference between showing someone how to do a problem and simply giving the answer. Discussion about this problem, lessons on helping, and role playing are ways to teach effective helping.

On occasion, helpers can be trained and even certified. One third-grade teacher trains students in the proper use of audiovisual equipment. Only students with an operator's license can operate the equipment.

TAPE RECORDER LICENSE

_____Record   _____Rewind

_____Play   _____Plug in
earphones

_____Fast forward   _____Stop

This form means that _____ has been
checked out on the tape recorder and is trained as a Tape
Recorder Operator.

_____   _____
Date   Signature of Teacher

A Helping Directory is another way to organize helpers. Brainstorm with students several categories in which help might be desired and given during the year—math, spelling, art, sports, fixing things, maps, music. Create a notebook with a page for each category. Students who see themselves as possible helpers in each category sign their names on that page and describe how they can be helpful. Later, when a child wants help in math, she looks up math in the directory and finds several names of people willing to help.

Some situations call for a committee of experts. When you publish student writing, use an editing committee. It's the committee's responsibility to notice errors in spelling and punctuation and request revisions. They also approve or reject submissions.

Putting other experts to use in your classroom communicates to students that you are not the source of all knowledge. As the year goes on, students widen their view of what and who they see as available resources. They increasingly see themselves and one another as resources that are able, capable, and useful. You can imagine what happens to their feelings of power and potency!

Guidance Forms

Use and display guidance forms and examples of appropriate work around the room in an effort to make yourself dispensable. If students are learning cursive, put a cursive alphabet on display. That way students don't have to keep coming to you for help and they can be more self-responsible.

If compositions are being written, post a composition guidance form. Show students on that form where you want their names and the date. Show them how paragraphs are indented, where the title goes, and where you expect to find the conclusion. Showcase any other of your expectations.

The composition guidance form is an invitation and is there to help students help themselves. Explain that you'll be taking their papers home to correct and that you'll be looking for the items listed on the composition guidance form. If students accept the invitation and check over their own papers first, they can use the guidance form. The form is an opportunity for them to guide themselves.

If you have expectations for the library corner or the bathroom pass or journal writing, display those guidelines in appropriate places. Of course, you do go over the guidelines and give all those directions verbally, but students do forget, do tune out, are absent, and don't always pay attention. By having directions and expectations posted in full view, you eliminate the need for students to come to you. You have invited them to partake of one more experience at being responsible for themselves and solving their own problems. In addition, you have made yourself more dispensable.

SELF-MONITORING

An additional strategy for inviting student responsibility is to structure self-monitoring experiences into your classroom management scheme. Self-monitoring activities require children to observe their progress over time. The activities can be academic or social and are created by structuring in processes that involve self-checking, self-evaluation (see Chapter 6), record keeping, or time budgeting.

Involving children in monitoring their own progress and growth does two things for them. First, it invites students to behave responsibly and see themselves as responsible. Second, it communicates to them that *they* are responsible for their own learning. It lets students know that you believe they are so responsible for their learning that they are expected to keep track of some of that learning.

Self-Checking

Self-checking activities are another way of making yourself dispensable. Teachers who check every paper and every problem are making themselves indispensable. Their students begin to believe that it's the teacher's job to correct papers, record scores, and monitor progress. Children learn that it's their job to do the work and someone else's job to monitor it. The result is dependency.

When you arrange things so that students can correct and record some of their own efforts, you send them a different message. You communicate that students are responsible, you communicate trust, and you communicate that the emphasis in our classroom is on learning rather than on right answers.

If you correct all work yourself and keep continuous records of right and wrong, you take the emphasis away from learning and put it on right answers. Children learn quickly that right answers are what's important. They then rush to accumulate as many right answers as possible.

In math it's important to know which students have mastered the skill of re-ordering numerals, for example, and which ones haven't. You don't have to check ten days' worth of four rows of problems per day to make that determination. You can do it with a quick quiz or with a red-dot system. When a group of students gets to a red-dot page in the math book, that's a signal for a mini-checkup on the material. You can set them down and give them a half-page ditto with five problems on it. By observing what students do on that ditto, you can determine whether or not they are ready to go on to the next skill level. The emphasis continues to be on mastery and learning, not on accumulating row after row of correct answers.

Concern. What if I create self-checking materials and kids cheat? What if they look at the answers?

Reply. When you put out self-checking activities for children, explain that the emphasis is on learning not on right answers. When students work on math facts using a self-checking device and they don't know an answer, encourage them to look. Tell them to look as often as they want until they feel they've learned the fact. Then have them repeat the activity. If they still need to look, tell them to look some more. What you have done is legitimatize looking. You have made it legal. It's now OK for students to look because learning is stressed rather than accumulating right answers.

Also, there is no longer a need to cheat. If mastery is required, cheating doesn't get the cheater anywhere. In fact it delays mastery. Students who learn that cheating doesn't get them anywhere have no reason to cheat.

Time Budgeting

Time budgeting is another area in which students can assume some responsibility. In many classrooms teachers decide when each activity begins and ends. Students follow the teacher's time sequencing and move from one task to another on command. In other classrooms a schedule of assignments for the morning is explained and students work on them in any order. Students have considerable experience in choosing how to budget their time. They learn lessons in math and social studies, but they also learn lessons in time budgeting.

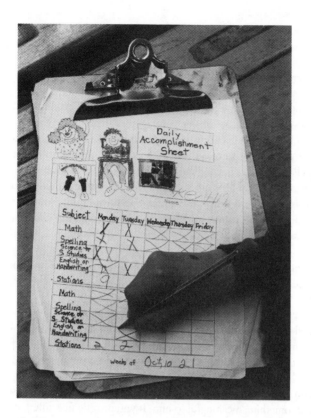

Students come to you with different skill levels in time budgeting. Some appear unable to handle even the smallest amount of time constructively. Others plan an entire day, stay on task, and complete their goals.

Time budgeting is learned the same way that other skills are learned, through teaching lessons, opportunities to practice, feedback on the effort, guidance and direction, and more opportunities to practice. Begin with small amounts of time and limited choices for students whose time-budgeting skills are low. Increase length of time and number of choices as students' skills increase.

CHOICE MAKING

The issue of choice is important to inviting student responsibility. Offering students a choice invites them to exercise control and participate in self-management. Choice-making opportunities enable children to experience and see the control they have.

The simple act of choosing strengthens children's feelings of ownership. If children have a choice and are aware of that choice, they feel they cause what they did. If they don't have a choice are less likely to believe that they are the cause. When students perceive themselves as the cause and in control, they are less likely to resist and act reluctant.

A reason for taking class time to help students learn choice making is that the choice-making process is a key factor in our participatory democracy. Each day the political, business, and educational leaders of our country make choices that affect us and our offspring for generations to come. That seems reason enough to help all our citizens learn the skills involved in making meaningful, appropriate decisions.

Choice making is a critical life skill. Your students are already, or will soon be, facing important decisions on sex, drugs, careers, and personal health. As adults they will deal with constant choice-making situations in terms of finance, child rearing, life-style, and other issues. The need to make choices doesn't go away. It's a lifelong process.

Giving children opportunities to make choices is also a useful method for making yourself dispensable. It's a way of sharing control by letting students in on a piece of the action.

The simple act of choosing between two alternatives can be a powerful motivator. If a child can choose the state on which to write a report, or which method of planting to use for her seeds, or which partner to work with during spelling study time, it is more likely that she will choose to act motivated and concerned.

Any time you increase the number of choices a child has, you increase the chance that he'll find something meaningful to him. If you provide five different story starters, he can probably find one he sees as exciting. If only one is provided, you run a greater risk of the student choosing disinterest or boredom.

Controlled Choices

Choices can be overdone, however. Too many choices blow kids' minds. I worked with a kindergarten teacher who experienced this problem during Choice Time. As she described it, "Kids were running around leaving messes, being loud, and disturbing each other." They flitted from one activity to another and did not get into any activity in depth. The situation got so bad that this teacher considered eliminating Choice Time as part of the day.

I listened patiently as she described her problem. When she finished I asked, "What are the choices that kids have during Choice Time?" Her reply, "Oh, they can do anything they want to." And indeed they could. Nothing was off limits. The five-year-olds could get out any puzzle, any library book, any game. They could play in the dress-up corner and use any of the props. Blocks, cars, paints, scissors and paste, as well as leftover snacks were all among the unlimited choices available.

These children were clearly having difficulty focusing and getting involved in depth because there were too many choices. The solution was not in eliminating Choice Time but rather in restructuring it to limit the choices. Choices controlled by the teacher so that students could pick from limited alternatives turned out to be more within these children's ability to focus and concentrate.

Another advantage of structuring choices is that *you* control the choices. If students can do anything that they want to, you have no control over how they spend that time. That's not *shared* control. It is *child* control.

With a controlled choice structure, you arrange choices that enhance what you're trying to accomplish in your classroom. You put out materials that reinforce the skills and concepts students have been working on. And you arrange choices to precue content that will be taught in the next few weeks as a preview of coming attractions.

Controlled choice also helps games and materials retain their appeal. Children get tired of Scrabble if they can play it any time and any day that they choose. But if it disappears and is not an option for a few weeks then it's like new again when it reappears.

A fifth-grade teacher I worked with had spent time during the summer making a shoebox art learning center. He obtained thirty shoeboxes and filled each with a different art activity. Within the boxes were file cards with directions, all materials that were needed, and evaluation forms. The project was impressive.

Early in the school year he shared his summer's effort with students. He explained the shoebox art activities and a procedure for using them. The students loved the area—for about two weeks. Then they were done.

After two weeks these children had seen it all. They had completed the art activities they were most interested in and rejected the others as dull and uninteresting. Their initial enthusiasm had ended.

This teacher was sick. He found it difficult to believe that a project he had spent so much time to create could be over so quickly. As he shared his concern with me, he began to realize that he had structured too many choices. He had put out all thirty choices at once. The "interesting" choices were quickly completed, the children were finished.

This teacher vowed to do it differently the next year. And indeed he did! When school began in the fall, children found four shoebox art activities in the art center. As interest in the four choices waned, he gradually replaced them with the other twenty-six. This style of structuring the choices had students doing art projects for eleven weeks. Controlled choice, in this case, was a much wiser use of the teacher's time and energy. And the children ended up doing more art.

Choosing as a Skill

Another consideration when structuring choices for children is to remember that choice-making is a skill. And as such it can be learned, strengthened, and improved upon. Children come to us with a wide range of choice-making abilities. Some (whose parents don't value choice making) come to school with practically no experience in choosing. These parents make most of the decisions, so their children arrive at school with a limited history in choice making and few opportunities to experience the consequences of their choices. Naturally their skills are limited.

Other parents allow children to make choices if the choices are "correct." These parents protect children by not letting them make "poor" choices and deprive them of experiencing the direct results of those choices.

Still other children come from homes where parents value the choosing process. They have had many opportunities to experience choice making and to learn from their choices.

Some students might not make positive, helpful choices right away or all the time. In learning any new skill, children sometimes do it poorly before they learn to do it well. Positive, healthy choice making doesn't always occur just because you've decided to invite children to choose. Children make mistakes with choice making the same way they make mistakes in math. Hang in there. Process those mistakes and help children learn from them. It's worth the effort. Remember, children won't improve without practice.

Structure initial choices so that students experience a degree of success. Ability levels must be taken into account. If each alternative is outside the ability level of the student, then there is no choice. Moderate difficulty is the rule for structuring initial choice-making experiences. Keep the choices easy enough that students can experience success, but not so easy that there is no challenge.

Availability of Choices

Making choices available to children is a simple process. It is as simple as placing three magazine pictures on a bulletin board and asking students to pick one as a writing topic. It is as uncomplicated as assigning six rows of math problems and requiring students to choose any three rows to complete. Other possibilities follow.

1. Each week make a list of the "significant happenings." Invite a committee to choose which items to place in "Our Class History Book."

2. Each week create three different spelling lists. Gear them for different ability levels. Label them "Words for Super Spellers," "Words for OK Spellers," and

"Words for Troubled Spellers." Let students choose which list they feel is appropriate for their own ability level.

3. Let children decide where to sit.

4. Have students choose reading partners.

5. Ask students to decide whether to take unfinished work home or complete it during recess.

6. Let students determine the criteria to be used to decide on a class play.

7. Write the morning agenda on the board. Invite children to decide which assignment to do first, second, and third.

8. Put several quotations on the board.

☆ None of us is as smart as all of us.
☆ I gotta be me.
☆ Today is the first day of the rest of my life.

Ask students to read the quotations, choose one that has meaning to them, and write about it.

9. Collect shopping bags from businesses. Get one each from a fast-food restaurant, a record shop, a food store, a pharmacy, a department store, a pizza place, and others. Have students choose one bag and write about it. Some possibilities include

☆ My first day on the job
☆ How to make_____
☆ What's your bag?

10. Ask students to study the choices they make concerning their own behavior. They pick any three of the following and write their reactions.
How do you change your behavior when

☆ You have company for dinner
☆ Your mother is sick
☆ You have had to sit too long in one position
☆ Your grandparents visit
☆ You stay overnight at a friend's house

11. Make a chart of "Things to Do When You Finish Your Work." Let students who finish early choose from that list. Some examples are

- ☆ Read quietly
- ☆ Clean out your desk
- ☆ Do puzzles
- ☆ Do brain teasers
- ☆ Others

12. On occasion, have students choose materials to use. For example, "Choose any three crayons to make a picture. Choose *only* three."

Choices and Shared Control

I recently observed a teacher using clothespins to offer students a library choice. A sign hung near the door. It read, "Library passes, good for fifteen minutes." Four clothespins were attached. Students wishing to use the library took a clothespin, attached it to their clothing, and left the room.

This is a prime example of shared control. To students it looked like they were in control—they got to decide when they wanted to go to the library. The clothespins were a visible reminder to them of their power.

Clearly students have a lot of control in this situation, yet not as much as might appear at first glance. Look at the control you, as the teacher, have in this situation. Your first choice is whether or not to give children any choice at all. Once you've decided to give choice, then you choose what form those choices are going to take.

If you show a filmstrip on South America and you want everyone present, going to the library is not a choice. Don't put the library passes (clothespins) out. You control that option.

On the other hand, maybe you're having a Choice Time during the afternoon. Some children are finishing art projects. Others are choosing math-oriented skill games. Still others are reading in the quiet corner. If this is an appropriate time for some students to choose the library, put the clothespins out.

Another choice you have is the number of clothespins to put out. Maybe you're not comfortable with four students leaving the room at one time. Perhaps only two students being gone fits more within your comfort zone. You decide that number. Create it the way you want it.

Time is another factor you control. Is fifteen minutes too long for you? How about ten? Again, it's your choice.

Another choice you have is to remove the privilege from those who abuse it. If two or three students are not acting responsibly on the way to the library, then they are likely to lose the privilege. Abuse it, you lose it!

The library pass structure appears to students as if they decide. They see the choice and they experience exercising control over their school lives. Yet you maintain control by the choices you make in structuring the situation. You are in control. The students are in control. You are feeling powerful. The students are feeling powerful. That's one of the beauties of shared control. Everyone has power and everyone wins.

Choice and Response-ability

One way to look at responsibility is to write it this way—*response-ability*. Response-ability is the ability to make responses. Children who see only one response to a certain situation have limited response-ability. They aren't able to make many responses.

In computer language this situation is called "requisite variety." In requisite variety the computer program with the most alternatives always wins. If one has four options and another has five options, the program with five options eventually wins. It has a greater ability to respond. It has response-ability.

It's the same with children. Children who sense more choices in a situation are more likely to come out winners. They have a greater repertoire of potential behaviors from which to choose. The children who see a limited number of responses, or who always respond the same way to a situation, end up as losers. Children who perceive only one response to a situation have little response-ability. They are immobilized by their limited awareness of choices.

One of the major roles of anyone who works with children is to help them see the choices available to them. If a child is not aware of a choice, she has no choice. Part of effective classroom management is helping children see meaningful alternatives to their behavior. It is a way of inviting them to be responsible.

If an eight-year-old is on the playground and some kids grab his hat and run, he has a choice of several behaviors. He can run after the offenders calling names, ignore them, tattle, persuade other students to help him, take something of theirs, wait until later and share his feelings with them, write them a note, sit down and cry, or any other number of possible behaviors. But those choices are only available to him if he is aware that they exist.

One of the mistakes educators often make is assuming that children see the choices. It isn't always so. Many times children see only one response to a situation and choose that same response over and over again even though it seldom works.

Monday	They grab his hat.	He calls them names.	He gets slugged.
Tuesday	They grab his hat.	He calls them names.	He gets slugged.
Wednesday	They grab his hat.	He calls them names.	He gets slugged.

And he always ends up getting slugged. Now if they grab his hat on Thursday and he calls them names and gets slugged, perhaps you would say he's a slow learner. The problem is deeper than that. This child has no awareness of other choices. And until he gets some new insight or adds another response, chances are he won't break that pattern.

It is our job as educators to help students explore alternatives to their behavior. We have a responsibility to give guidance and direction. We can be helpful by listening, modeling, and pointing out to students responses that work. We can help students take a look to see if their behaviors are getting them what they want. We can help them brainstorm other ways of acting and let them choose ones they feel are appropriate.

The first time I walked into Ione Condit's classroom I noticed a huge chart on the wall. "Instead of Fighting" was the title. Five alternatives were listed for everyone to see.

☆ Talk it out—reason
☆ Take turns
☆ Get a referee
☆ Stay away from each other
☆ Pretend you're the other person

The chart, produced by and for children, was created to help students visualize the choices. It helped them see that fighting was not the only alternative in certain situations.

Ione had processed several fights at the beginning of the year. She had taken the time to help children talk things out and make peace with each other. The results of those talks were usually positive, but she was tired of processing the fights and was disturbed by their frequency.

Ione brought the problem to a class meeting. Children offered their suggestions of what to do instead of fighting. They then picked five they thought would work for them, and the chart was created. Each alternative was role played, discussed, and evaluated.

Role playing a new behavior helps students gauge the possible outcomes of that choice. It is also useful because it plants pictures of the alternatives in children's minds. Once children can see the alternatives, they become more likely to choose them in appropriate situations.

In the case of Ione's children, seeing the options helped. The list and the role plays did not eliminate fighting, but they reduced both the intensity and the frequency. When her students used one of the alternatives to fighting, they shared their experiences orally with the class. Feelings were explored as well as level of satisfaction. Congratulations and encouragement were extended by Ione and classmates. Children learned slowly, over time, to see that fighting isn't always the answer.

Perception of Choice

In many daily situations, children don't see themselves as responsible. They blame the other person ("He made me do it"). They disown ("It's not my fault"). In many cases children aren't aware at a conscious level that they are choosing. Our job as teachers is to confront them gently by pointing out the choice and bringing it to a conscious level.

If you tell children to leave a class meeting because of repeated distracting side conversations, students sometimes will react as though you made them leave. They believe that it was your choice. It's time to help students change their minds about that and see the connections between their behavior and the consequences. It's time to help students realize that they made the choice to leave the class meeting and that they have communicated that choice to you through their behavior. It's also time to help them know that they can make another choice and return when they choose to live by the rule of no side conversations.

Helping children see the choices they make is important. Verbalize to children the choices you see them make. Let them know *you* know they are choosing.

☆ You two boys have shown me by your behavior that *you have chosen* not to sit by each other for a while.

☆ I noticed that *you chose* to get angry during gym today, Marlene.

☆ If *you choose* to do it on the wrong side again, you'll have to do it over.

☆ How many of you *chose* to be prepared for the spelling test today?

☆ I'm wondering what grade *you will choose* to earn this semester.

☆ Sarah, I noticed when Bonnie teased you that *you chose* to ignore her.

Personalization of Choice

Another way to help children learn about choices is to study the issue and help them personalize it. When and where do children make choices in their lives? How do they feel about them? What meaning does making decisions have for them? Create tasks that help children explore their personal reactions to decision making. These can be done in writing or orally.

1. List five things that you got to decide this week. Put them in order of their importance to you.

2. Make a list of five things that other people decide for you that you would like to decide for yourself. Put them in order of their importance to you.

3. What are some things you get to decide now that you didn't get to when you were five years old. Pick one to tell about.

4. Are there some things you wish you didn't have to decide? List them. Pick one and write your reasons for not wanting to decide.

5. What decisions do you get to make at home? List five. Which decisions would you like to make at home? List five. Why do you think you should be allowed to make these decisions? Write out your reasons.

TEACHER BELIEFS ABOUT CHOICES

Where do you stand on the issue of choices? What are your beliefs? On a piece of paper mark your level of belief (scale of zero to ten) regarding the statements that follow. A zero indicates that you don't believe the statement at all. A ten indicates you believe the statement totally.

1. Children should be allowed to make choices.
2. Most children make positive choices.
3. Parents want their children to learn choice-making skills.
4. Creating choices is a lot of trouble for teachers. It takes more time than it's worth.
5. Students should learn to do the right thing when there is only one choice.
6. Students don't want to do any of the choices offered.

To compute your belief quotient for choice making, total your score for the first three beliefs. Then add the numbers of your last three beliefs. Subtract the total of your last three from the total of your first three.

> *Zero.* A score of zero indicates that you are equally split over the belief in the importance of choice making for children.
>
> *Above zero.* The higher your score the greater your belief in the importance of choice making for children.
>
> *Below zero.* The further your score goes below zero, the less you believe in the importance of choice making for children.

If you have a high score, then arranging choices for children will probably be exciting and rewarding for you. By arranging choices, your behavior will match your beliefs.

If you have a score significantly below zero, then arranging choices for children could be frustrating and unrewarding for you. In this case, it would be important for you to work at changing your beliefs along with changing your behavior of offering more choice-making opportunities to children.

Your classroom is an ongoing lab. It can be a lab where children learn obedience or one where they are issued continuous invitations to accept responsibility. The choice is yours.

Reread the portions of this chapter that hold special meaning for you. Underline three ideas you intend to implement. Write in the margin two others you thought of while reading the chapter. Share one with a colleague. Implement and enjoy the process. Do it now.

8

managing
my own mind

Teachers are managers. They manage furniture, equipment, classroom interactions, movement, content, masking tape, expectations, procedures, and processes in the learning environment. Although all of these are important, it may well be that the most important thing you, the teacher, have to manage is your mind. How you choose to manage and arrange your own mind greatly affects how you choose to manage all the other items under your control.

Teachers spend hour after hour working with students' minds, helping them think critically, form opinions, and make decisions. Yet it's a rare teacher who spends more than ten minutes a day working on his own mind, arranging it the way he wants, putting it in order to be useful and helpful.

Your mind is your greatest tool. It's a tool that will work *for* you or *against* you. You can use it to create a positive, warm classroom atmosphere or one that is cold and repressive. You can use it to produce happy, satisfied days or depressed, worn-out days. And you can use your mind to create an Our Classroom feeling.

Do you purposefully control your mind to enhance your teaching? Are you aware of connections between how you think and what you get from children and colleagues? Are you aware of how your mind creates the conditions that exist within your classroom? Do you believe you create your own reality?

WE CREATE OUR OWN REALITY

When I give workshops on "Using the Mind as a Management Tool" with teachers, I do an exercise in which I role-play an inept professor. I tell the participants that I am role playing and direct them to watch the scene because I'm going to ask them what they saw when I finish.

In the role I explain that this part of the training is the most important part to me. I share that I haven't yet found an effective way to deliver the content. I go on to tell how nothing I've done so far has worked and yet I believe that the message is critical. I inform participants I'm still struggling to find a way to share this content, which means so much to me.

I repeat myself, act nervous, stop in the middle of sentences, change direction, and generally act inept. After about three minutes of getting into the role, I end it.

At this point I ask people to report what they saw or felt. Typical reactions include

☆ I felt sorry for you.
☆ I saw a man confused.
☆ I noticed your honesty.
☆ You made me nervous for you.
☆ Oh, were you role playing?
☆ I just felt defeated when you said that no group had ever gotten it before.
☆ I felt the opposite. I considered it a challenge. I was ready to get it.
☆ I thought, "Oh, get on with it."
☆ I was bored.

Participants typically report some similarities in what they see and feel. Yet each person's response is different, each interpretation unique. The role-play situation is similar to an accident witnessed by several spectators—each has a different account of the accident. Each person comes away with a different version of reality.

We believe that we all create our own reality. We each perceive the events, situations, or people in our lives through our unique filters. Your filters are made up of your total life's experiences, values, and beliefs. When something happens in your life, you see it through your own private filters and make sense out of it through them. Because your filters are different from everyone else's, the reality you create for yourself is different from everyone else's.

Participants who view the professor role-play see it through their own filters. They pass it through their values, beliefs, and life experiences and come away with their own unique interpretations. What participants say they saw in the role play tells more about them than it does about what they saw.

Take *the day* for example. Some people say, "What a good day." Others remark, "What a crummy day." And it is the same day! The day isn't good or bad. The day just is. It simply comes to us as a day without evaluation attached to it.

The day isn't anything until you decide how it's going to be for you. If it's a good day for you it's because you've created it that way for yourself. If it's a bad day, then that too is because you've created it that way. How you choose to see the day tells a lot more about you than it does about the day.

Both of us love to run in the rain. We choose to see a light rainy day as exciting, exhilarating, and energy producing. When we run on those occasions, we seldom see anyone outside walking, running, or playing.

One afternoon we were out running in a light rain and it changed to a heavy downpour. The rain came straight down in torrents. We decided to enjoy what we were given and chose to see the downpour as positive.

We were alternately jumping over and running through puddles when we came around a corner of a carport to find an unexpected sight. A young mother and her year-old child were sitting in the middle of a huge puddle, totally wet and obviously happy. They were splashing and laughing, enjoying the rain and each other. We waved, smiled, and ran on as we splashed through the same puddle.

We saw no one else outside as we completed our forty-five-minute run. To others who had chosen to stay inside, it probably seemed like a bad day. To us and the young mother and child, it was a beautiful day! We had created our own reality.

We create our own reality in the classroom too—by how we *choose* to see children, by how we *choose* to see the learning process, and by how we *choose* to see all the events in our professional lives.

Take the example of spilled paint. Spilled paint is not good. Spilled paint is not bad. It's just spilled paint. And it stays spilled paint until we choose to think something about it. As a teacher you can choose to see spilled paint as a catastrophe or as an opportunity. You can believe that spilled paint is awful or you can believe that it is a chance to help students learn cooperative skills. You can arrange your mind to see spilled paint in a variety of ways.

You can't control all the events in your life, but you always control how you choose to *see* those events. And when an event like spilled paint occurs, you can choose how you want to perceive it—perception is a choice not a given.

Of course you attempt to prevent certain events. You put paint in low, flat containers instead of high, tippy ones. You limit the number of people working at the paint area at any given time to three students. That helps, and less paint is spilled. Yet regardless of how carefully you try to control and limit that event in your life, there are still times when paint gets spilled.

Knowing that you are in control of how you choose to see the events in your life is important, because how you react to those events depends on how you've chosen to see and think about them. What you *do* about spilled paint flows from how you choose to see and think about spilled paint.

If you perceive spilled paint as a *catastrophe*, you act out one set of behaviors. If you perceive spilled paint as an *opportunity*, you act out a different set. In each case the way you behave depends on your perception, and the perception you've chosen depends on how you've arranged your mind.

If you see spilled paint as awful, you enact blame and punishment behaviors. You find out who did it, impose an appropriate punishment, and act angry. If you see spilled paint as an opportunity, you use problem-solving behaviors. You find out who is willing to help, search for immediate and long-range solutions, and act concerned. In each case behaviors evolve from how you choose to perceive the situation.

In Chapters 6 and 7 we detailed strategies for sharing control with students. What was your reaction to those strategies? How did you choose to see them? Did you see them as positive, helpful, and good or useless, negative, and bad? Chances are that how you choose to see shared control reveals more about you than it does about shared control. Shared control is not good. Shared control is not bad. It has no meaning until you attach one to it.

Self-checking materials are one way to share control with students. Occasionally students use the opportunity and the self-checking materials to give themselves answers. That is typically referred to as cheating.

What teachers do about cheating depends on how they choose to see cheating. If they believe that cheating is terrible, intolerable, and to be avoided at all costs, they employ "cheat control" behaviors. They don't use self-checking materials. They have students sit with their desks far apart. They tell them that they must keep their eyes on their own papers and that they'll get zeroes if they're caught looking. Behavior follows beliefs.

On the other hand, teachers who believe that cheating is an opportunity for someone to learn about cheating, or that it is a cry for help, employ problem-solving behaviors. They talk with the child privately, confront the situation, and engage in a mutual search for a solution. They stay positive, disdain punishment, and continue to move toward finding solutions. Again, behavior follows beliefs.

There are two points here—that there is a connection between how you arrange your mind and how you behave as a teacher, and that arranging your mind is a choice, something over which you have control. If you arrange your mind one way, you behave that way. If you arrange your mind another way, then you behave that way. It all starts with how you choose to arrange your mind.

THE EVENT-RESPONSE MODEL

Our friends Diane Blecha and Tim Timmermann have constructed a visual model to help explain the concept of arranging your mind. They call it the "Event–Response model."[1]

Some people believe that the events of our lives *cause* our responses. In the Event-Response model that belief looks like this (see page 110).

[1]Tim Timmermann and Diane Blecha, *Modern Stress: The Needless Killer* (Dubuque, IA: Kendall Hunt Publishing Company, 1982), p. 56.

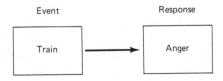

A train stops me on my way to school. I know that I'm going to be late for a staff meeting and my response is one of anxiety and anger. The train "makes me" angry.

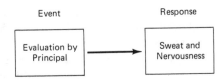

My principal comes in, sits in the back of my room, and starts writing. I know it's teacher evaluation time. I start to get nervous. The principal "makes me" nervous.

It looks like cause and effect, doesn't it? It looks as though in each case the event causes the response. That's how "makes me" language comes into play.

But something is missing there. Not all people react the same way to a train slowing their drive to school. Not all people get nervous and sweat when the principal starts evaluation procedures. "Makes me" language and the apparent cause and effect relationships are not accurate. Let's take a closer look.

Diane and Tim explain that when an event happens, "there is a part of every person that gets triggered, gets put to work, becomes engaged. That part is the part of every human that gives meaning to the event. Although 20 people all see or experience the same thing, they may derive vastly different meanings from them."[2] That is exactly what happened with my role play of the inept professor.

The Interpretive Mind

The part of us that becomes engaged is the *interpretive mind*—the part that gives the event meaning. The interpretive mind occupies a crucial place in the Event–Response model. What actually happens is a three-step process: (1) A person experiences an

[2]Ibid., p. 67.

110

event, (2) her mind interprets that event, and (3) she makes a response. The diagram now looks like this.

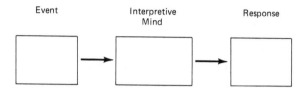

The interpretive mind functions in three ways to create a response to the events of a person's life. Responses to events are results of the interpretive mind engaging a *belief,* holding on to a *thought,* or holding on to an *image.*

Let's go back to the train as an event and plug it into the new model.

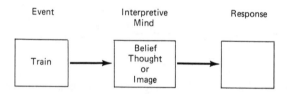

The train pulling in front of my path ensuring that I will be late for the morning staff meeting is the event. Next, my mind interprets that event with a belief, a thought, or an image. If my *belief* is that people shouldn't be late, my response is irritation. If I hold an *image* in my mind of my principal and colleagues turning their heads to look at me as I enter and I imagine frowns on their faces, then my response to the train is anxiety. If my *thought* is "My principal is not going to like this," my response is tension.

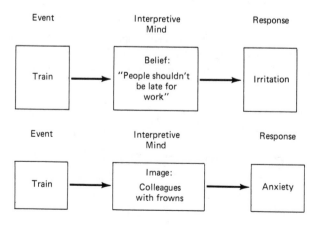

On the other hand, my mind can make a variety of other more helpful interpretations. I can elect to engage more useful thoughts, images, and beliefs.

My thought can be "This train is a signal to me to slow down. I've been running too fast." If that's my thought, then my response is to relax by doing some deep breathing.

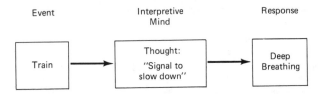

Another thought I can choose is "I'm glad the train stopped me. I can use ten minutes to prepare my committee report for the staff meeting." Then my response is ten minutes of planning.

Perhaps one of my beliefs is "What happens, happens, and I make the best of it." If that belief becomes engaged then I choose a response like doing isometric exercises, writing in my journal, or listing five things that I want to do today.

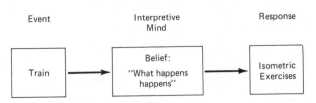

The point we want to emphasize here is that the event does not *cause* the response. *I* cause the response by the thought, belief, or image I choose to hold on to in any given situation, and that is my choice.

The train does not *make me* angry. *I* make me angry by the thoughts that I choose to think about the train. The principal in the back of my room does not *make me* nervous. *I* make me nervous by the images I put in my mind or the thoughts I think about my principal being there. And because I am in control of the thoughts, images, and beliefs that are in my mind at any given time, I am in control of how I react to the events of my life. Again, I create my own reality.

Situation 3

Consider the following situation. You're in the teachers' room enjoying your lunch, eating at a leisurely pace, and relaxing on your only break of the day. There's a knock on the door. It's the playground supervisor. She has two boys from your room, a collar in each hand. "They've been kicking and fighting," she explains as she deposits them by the door.

What is your response? Do you get angry? Do you have the boys wait outside until you're finished eating? Do you listen to their stories, fix blame, and mete out punishment? Or do you tell them to sit there on the floor and talk it over until they solve their own problem? Do you go back to your lunch and complain about being interrupted? Do you send them to the principal? Do you call the parents? Whatever your response, be aware that it came about because of how you arranged your mind and how you chose to interpret the event.

The event is that two boys got into a fight on the playground in the middle of your lunch break. When this event occurs a variety of thoughts, images, or beliefs are possible. Some include

☆ Fighting is awful
☆ It isn't fair that my break is interrupted
☆ This is an opportunity to help them learn problem-solving skills
☆ People should talk out their problems
☆ These two sure are a challenge
☆ Those two will never learn

It's possible to think any one of these thoughts following the situation just described. And the choice of which one to hold on to is yours. *I* am responsible for the thoughts that *I* think. *You* are responsible for the thoughts that *you* think. No one can *make* either of us think a thought. That is under our control. We are all responsible for our own thoughts. It's one way we create our own reality.

The schematic diagram helps explain how different thoughts, beliefs, or images result in different behaviors. First a situation occurs.

```
   Situation
Two Boys Fighting
```

To make sense out of that "happening" the interpretive mind takes over. The mind chooses a thought or an image to hold on to or engages a belief. In the case of the two boys fighting, thoughts could be "This is awful" or "This is a chance to help them."

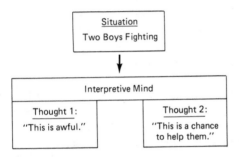

The way the mind interprets the situation affects how you see the situation. If your thought is "This is awful," then you're likely to perceive the boys as trouble-makers. On the other hand, if your thought is "This is a chance to help them," you're more likely to perceive the situation as a cry for help.

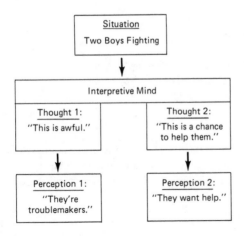

Next, your perception affects the action you take. How you *see* the situation influences what you *do* about the situation. The diagram now looks like this.

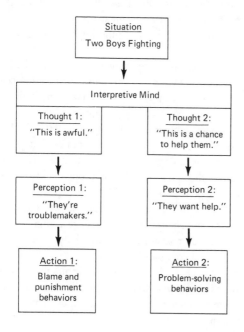

In this diagram there is only one situation. Yet because two different interpretations are made, different perceptions result and different actions follow.

Points of Control

Concern. You talk about interpreting events and situations as if I have a choice. My mind doesn't think about it consciously. My perception just happens.

Reply. What you are suggesting is that you are not aware of the choice you make. Actually there are several places in this diagram where you can make a choice and take control.

Maybe you believe thoughts just pop into your head without any choice on your part. Even if that were accurate, you still have the choice to pop those thoughts right back out once you notice them. A technique to use is to say to yourself, "That's one way to think about it. Now what's another way?"

Thoughts come and go. When a thought comes that you don't like, let it go and let another thought come in to replace it. Don't hold tightly to any thought that is not useful to you. Select thoughts that leave you in a place you like.

This is how it works for me. If I am doing a workshop for teachers and only ten people show up, a thought may pop into my head, "Teachers just don't care about their own professional development any more." That's not a helpful thought. I can also think, "Wow! These ten people must really want to be here!" Now that's the kind of thought I want to hold in my mind. That's the kind of thought from which I want my behavior to flow.

Selecting useful thoughts begins with noticing them as they occur. Perhaps, though, you aren't in the habit of monitoring your thoughts and you don't notice the thoughts you have. You still have another point of choice. That point is the perception stage.

Maybe you're more aware of what you *see* than of what you *think*. By being aware of your perception, you can also make a choice. If you notice that you are seeing your students as troublemakers, for example, you can use that as a clue to re-examine your thoughts. Ask yourself the question, "What thoughts have I been having that are producing this unhelpful perception?"

If you catch yourself at this stage with a negative perception, you're now in a position to do something about it. You can change your mind by rearranging it with new thoughts and images. Yes, you can rearrange your mind by changing the thought, image, or belief that has produced your perception!

There is still another point of choice available to you. It occurs in the action phase. Let's assume you missed your thought and weren't aware of it. Let's assume also that you missed your perception and weren't aware of it either. You can still catch yourself if you notice your action.

Perhaps one day you're in the middle of screaming at your class and you notice your behavior. Or perhaps you notice that your stomach is all tied up in knots. Or maybe you catch yourself using sarcasm. In each case, you have noticed your behavior. That's an important first step, because now you can do something about it.

When you catch yourself doing an action that you don't like or one that is not useful, stop and ask yourself, "How am I doing this to myself? What kinds of thoughts am I thinking that produce this behavior in me?"

Chances are if you hear yourself being sarcastic with children, you're probably seeing them in some evaluative way. Let's say you're choosing to interpret their inactive behavior as lazy. If you're perceiving children as lazy then your thought may have been "Doing nothing is a waste of time" or "Kids should always be busy."

Your perception and your action flowed from your thoughts. To change your action of being sarcastic, alter your thoughts. You manage your own mind. Rearrange it by putting thoughts in there that lead to actions that are positive and helpful to you.

As you can see, you have several opportunities to be in control of your mind. You can decide which thought to put in your mind in the first place. Having missed that point of control, you can change your thought once you become aware of it. If you miss that choice point, you still have two more opportunities for awareness and control. It's possible to become aware of your perception or of your behavior. Noticing those will provide you with still more chances to take control and rearrange your mind.

We all have the capacity to manage our own minds. Why not manage yours in a way that leaves you in a place you like? You create your own reality. Why not create it the way you like it?

THE CLASSROOM
AS A LABORATORY

One way Our Classroom teachers arrange their minds is to see classrooms as labs—labs in responsibility and labs in cooperation. By *lab* we mean the typical laboratory definition, as in *science lab*.

Science labs are purposefully set up so children have experiences that invite them to learn through the process of mistakes, adjustments, and rediscovery. I remember working with a partner in eighth-grade science class using batteries, wires, and bulbs. We were trying to get the bulb to light up. We would touch certain wires to the bulb and battery and then observe. Nothing. We'd try other wires. Still nothing. Finally, after several tries, we stumbled onto the right combination. The bulb went on. We wrote that down in our workbooks and proceeded to the next step.

The lab was set up so that we learned from our mistakes. Mistakes weren't veiwed as bad. They were simply seen as one of the steps in the process of learning.

One way to look at the classroom is to see it as a lab in responsibility. As a teacher it's possible for you to see the classroom as a series of responsibility-practicing situations. If you arrange your mind to perceive the classroom that way, then you create situations where children practice responsibility. You help them process and learn from their mistakes, and you create more situations for children to practice.

You can choose to see classrooms as labs where children learn lessons in responsibility or you can choose to see classrooms as places where mistakes in responsibility are not supposed to happen. Either way, your behavior follows your perception.

If you arrange your mind to perceive classrooms as places where mistakes in responsibility are not supposed to happen, then you allow children few chances to exercise responsibility. You allow few mistakes because you allow few chances for children to practice. You enact blame and punishment behaviors and get disgusted when children make mistakes.

Seeing the classroom as a lab in cooperation is another way that Our Class-room practitioners arrange their minds. These teachers behave to reflect that view.

They create opportunities for students to practice and they purposefully structure the interaction patterns so that children experience specific cooperative skill lessons. The teachers observe, give direct feedback to children, and design more cooperative lessons. (This cooperative group structure has become so refined that we are devoting Chapter 9 to its definition and implementation.)

EXPECTATION

Research is clear on the importance of teachers' expectations. Numerous studies document the relationship between what teachers expect and what they get (the self-fulfilling prophecy). Teachers who have high expectations of children behave differently toward those children than they do toward those for whom they have lower expectations. Teachers are more encouraging toward students they believe have high potential and are more discouraging to those they believe do not have high potential. When teacher expectations are high, teachers demand better performance from students and praise that performance more often. On the opposite side, teachers accept a poor performance more often from the children they see as having low potential and are less inclined to praise a good performance by those children even when it occurs.

The message here seems clear enough—teachers get what they expect. If you expect children to achieve, they achieve. If you expect them to act out, they act out. If you expect them to cooperate, they cooperate.

We believe there are two reasons why you get what you expect. First, your behaviors change with your expectations. If you believe that children are intelligent and capable of rapid learning, you behave differently toward them. Your behavior change is not always conscious; it is often subtle. Children pick up on those behavioral clues whether they are communicated verbally or nonverbally. Over time they come to understand and fall in line with your expectations.

Another reason you get what you expect is because you prove your beliefs to yourself. If you believe students are incapable of solving their own problems intelligently, you prove that to yourself by noticing all those times when they choose unwise solutions. You expect unwise solutions so you unconsciously look for them. And because you're looking for them you notice them more often. And the more you see them the more you believe students will choose unwise solutions. And you continue to get what you expect.

If you believe that children are cooperative, you're more likely to notice acts of cooperation. If you believe that students are uncooperative you're more likely to notice uncooperative acts. You tend to filter out messages that do not fit with your beliefs.

Our Classroom teachers realize the power inherent in expectation. And they realize their power to choose the expectation they wish. Expectation is never fixed—it is always a choice. Our Classroom teachers carefully choose their expectations about children, coworkers, and themselves to create results that are satisfying. It's one more way they manage their own minds and one more way they create their own realities.

You can believe that students care about one another and expect them to act that way, or you can believe that students don't care about one another and expect them to act *that* way. The choice of belief and expectation is yours. And the choice is critical, because whatever belief you choose to hold on to (cause) helps create what you get as a result (effect).

What you expect is what you look for. What you look for is what you see. What you see is what you get. And what you get is what you expect in the future.

What do you expect from the children you work with? Are you expecting them to act responsibly or to act out? Do you have high or low expectations for their academic achievement? Do you know what your expectations are?

One way to get in touch with your expectations is to take a close look at what you're getting. Because you get what you expect, examining what you're getting tells a great deal about what your expectations have been in the past. You can change what you get from students by arranging your mind to expect the behaviors, attitudes, and achievement that you desire. Begin today to get what you really want from teaching. What is it that you want? Make a list now.

Next turn these wants into expectations. Expect them. Look for them. Dwell on them. Believe that they will happen for you. Notice them.

Each morning after you awaken and before you rise, picture your expectations. See in your mind what it will look like when your expectations have materialized in your classroom. Observe the completion of your expectations. Feel the emotion of success and having it the way you want it. Enjoy the pictures and the feelings. Do this positive picturing for several minutes.

Then get up and forget it. Just let it go and trust that it will happen. When you get to the classroom "act as if" what you want already exists. Pretend that it's already happening. Assume that children will act the way you expect them to behave. Assume that children will achieve the way you expect them to achieve. Be openly surprised if an incident occurs that is in conflict with your expectation.

Persist in arranging your mind with the expectations you want and marvelous changes will occur. You will immediately begin to notice small changes. Use those initial changes as times to congratulate yourself. Already your mind is working for you, producing the results you want. Know that more are coming. Even the greatest rivers begin with the tiniest trickles. Believe that the rush is starting. Feel positive and be appreciative of what you have started.

AFFIRMATIONS

An affirmation is a positive thought you have purposely chosen to plant in your mind to produce a result you desire. It is a technique Our Classroom teachers use to arrange their own minds and create their own realities.

Our Classroom teachers believe their minds are powerful. They believe their minds will create whatever they want if given a chance. Affirmations are one way they give their minds a chance.

Examples of affirmations follow.

☆ I run effective class meetings in which children see themselves as able problem solvers.

☆ I view students positively and communicate that view to them.

☆ I see classroom problems as opportunities and welcome them for the solutions they produce.

☆ I notice opportunities to help children validate their strengths.

☆ I notice that children are capable of doing for themselves.

☆ I find time to include the classroom activities I feel are important.

☆ I think of numerous ways to enhance the self-concepts of the students in Our Classroom.

It is possible to imprint your subconscious mind through repetitious thought. Using affirmations is a way to do that. Once an affirmation has made its impression on your subconscious mind, your old thought pattern will be replaced with the new affirmed thought. Because creating a new habit takes time, the following steps are necessary to create what you desire.

1. *Use all your senses.* Say the affirmation to yourself. Hear it out loud. Repeat it in front of a mirror. Put it on a tape and play it back. Taste it, touch it, feel it if you can.

2. *Be selective.* Work on one to three affirmations at a time. Ten is too many. Concentrate and focus your attention on a limited number.

3. *Regularity.* Get in the habit of saying and writing your affirmations at the same time each day. Say them in the car on your way to work, at noon while you relax after lunch, or while you complete your evening run. An effective time to repeat affirmations is right before you go to sleep or right after you wake up. This is when your conscious and subconscious mind are closest. During that semi-dreamlike state between sleep and wakefulness it's easier to sink thoughts into your subconscious.

4. *After confirmation.* A particularly strong affirmation is said or written immediately following confirmation. If you are affirming "I think of numerous ways to en-

hance the self-concept of the students in Our Classroom" and you discover a new self-concept resource book, that's an appropriate time to affirm. That's a time when your belief is strongest and your affirmation carries the most power.

Here are some examples.

☆ Affirm "I run effective class meetings" right after you and the children have solved a sticky problem together.

☆ Affirm "I view students positively and communicate that view to them" after you have created a Proud Board where children showcase their successes.

☆ Affirm "I find time to include the classroom activities I feel are important" at the end of a day when you achieve your goals.

5. Images and visualizations. The suconscious mind is impressed with images. The words, the verbal and linear quality of writing and speaking, are left-brain activities. Images and pictures are right-brain activities. Get both sides of your brain working together in harmony. Affirmations are more powerful when there is a visual image associated with the words. It is important that the image you see shows you in your desired state.

If your affirmation is "I am a positive teacher," see yourself as positive. Picture the way you want to be. See your affirmation in the final state of completion. Notice how you concentrate on catching children being good. Picture yourself making positive comments. Visualize your self-talk as supportive and encouraging. See yourself smiling. Notice how you are appreciative of yourself and others.

If you affirm "I am organized and on time," put a picture of that in your mind. See yourself passing back student papers on schedule. Notice how organized your desk is. Plant that picture in your mind along with your affirmation.

One of my current affirmations is "I, Chick Moorman, am an author. I write a book that uplifts, illuminates, and helps others find direction in their lives." I have two images that go with my affirmation. One is the book itself. I see it clearly. In my mind I hold on to it, open it, and leaf through it. My second image is one of Dee and me autographing copies. I see us at workshops and in bookstores, happily signing our names as people purchase the book. The images strengthen my words and my beliefs.

6. Be patient. Persist in your mental work. It has taken you your whole life to get your mind to where it is now. You probably won't change it completely overnight. As you begin to work with affirmations, your subconscious mind may not believe them right away. It takes time to reprogram. Hang in there.

7. Be appreciative. Notice all signs of success. See them as signals that more is coming. If you are affirming seeing children positively and you notice that Jane told the truth about why she was fighting for the fourth time this week, rejoice in the signal that more positiveness is on the way. You can look at Jane, see the negative aspect of her fighting, and say, "I guess my affirmation is not working," or you can congratulate yourself for noticing the positive aspect that she told the truth. You can see your positive outlook as evidence of things to come. Think about it.

How Affirmations Work

Our sense of how affirmations work follows.

1. Affirmations and visualizations help us put pictures and thoughts of what we want in our minds.
2. The more we have these pictures and thoughts the more we expect them.
3. The more we expect them, the more we pay attention and notice them when they occur.
4. The more we notice them, the more we believe and expect them to happen. And the cycle continues to repeat itself.

Your Own Affirmations

Spend some time now designing affirmations for yourself. To begin this process, give some thought to what you want in your life. What is it you want to create for yourself as a teacher? Do you want happiness, growth for your students, a secure career, to be respected for the job you're doing? Any characteristic, condition, attitude, material object, outcome, or yearning can be affirmed into existence. What is it that *you* want?

Take the time now to brainstorm a list of fifteen things that you want in your life. They can be personal or professional. Include items like a close friendship, world travel, an advanced degree, children who listen, your perfect body weight, good health, humor, fame, compliments for the job you're doing, recognition, more time. List your fifteen now.

Now look over your list and put a star by the three that are most important to you. These are the three that are so important to you that you would be willing to spend some time each day attracting them into your life.

Now write an affirmation for each of the wants you starred. Design them like the examples in this chapter. Make them fit you. Be sure that your affirmations are written as if the condition you want already exists.

☆   I receive recognition for my efforts *not* People are beginning to notice my efforts.

☆   I run effective class meetings *not* I am capable of running effective class meetings.

☆   I am a positive teacher. I notice the good that exists in everything *not* I will be positive.

Write your affirmations now.

Now it's time to put a visual image with each affirmation. (Read the next two paragraphs before you begin.)

Relax, close your eyes and breathe deeply. Repeat your affirmation to yourself several times. Let an image appear in your mind's eye. This is a symbolic image that represents the completion of your desired want.

If you affirm recognition, see a newspaper article describing you as teacher of the year, or watch as your principal and colleagues give you compliments. If you affirm a cooperative group of children, see them helping one another, pulling together to achieve some common goal.

Autosuggestions

Another strategy Our Classroom practitioners use to create their own reality is autosuggestions. Autosuggestions are similar to affirmations only shorter. In fact, autosuggestions are short enough to qualify as (pardon the pun) bumper stickers.

Example of bumper stickers include

Do it now	Go for it
Act as if	It doesn't have to follow
Fake it till you make it	Take a full cut
I don't settle	I'm worth it
As one door closes another opens	I own my own stress

Bumper stickers are a method of programming the subconscious mind. Repeated use of a bumper sticker places it in your subconscious mind. Then, when you need it, that bumper sticker will flash into your awareness in time for you to use it.

I used to be a procrastinator. So a bumper sticker I chose to work with was "Do it now." I wrote that autosuggestion twenty times each morning for a week. That message sunk into my subconscious mind. My subconscious mind then sent the message back to my consciousness when it was helpful for me to "do it now."

I found that the more I listened to my subconscious mind, the more it worked for me. If I listened to the message "Do it now" and responded with action, then my mind continued to send the message. If I ignored the message and didn't act, then I didn't receive the message as often.

Pick a bumper sticker from this list or design one of your own to help arrange your own mind. Write it twenty times a day for a week and watch what happens. Listen for the message coming back and respond with action. If you abuse it, you'll lose it. If you respond, you'll strengthen it. You can create it the way you want it. The choice is yours.

We hope this chapter has helped you take a look at how you manage your own mind. The main idea is that we all create our own realities based on how we choose to see the people, events, and experiences of our lives. What we do about what happens in our lives depends greatly on how we choose to see what happens. We hope you have learned (or been reminded) that you have control over how you see and that you have a choice about how you manage your own mind.

9

managing the classroom for cooperation

Why can't these students get along with each other? Every time I ask them to do group work, there's trouble. They just won't cooperate.

I've tried groups and they don't work. Children don't get along with each other. Some never get involved. I give up!

The concerns above come from teachers we have worked with over the past several years. These teachers care about their students cooperating, getting along, and working together. Although their caring remains strong, they don't always know how to remedy the situation. When asked "How are you teaching cooperation?" most answer "The kids are just supposed to know." These teachers aren't sure what cooperation is, how it is created and maintained, or what skills are necessary to produce it.

Cooperation is a way of behaving that doesn't just happen. It does not occur by accident or by wishing it were there. For cooperation to occur in classrooms, teachers must take an active stance that includes a willingness to structure the environment to invite children to behave cooperatively. Cooperation comes as a result of teachers purposefully setting out to create it by structuring learning tasks in which children practice cooperative skills, learn from their mistakes and successes, and practice again. It comes from teachers who consciously choose to arrange the classroom interaction patterns so that children learn about cooperation. It comes from skilled teachers who deliver skills to children. And it happens on purpose.

NOTE: This chapter was written with help from our friend and colleague Pat Wilson O'Leary.

The cooperative learning model we recommend is designed by Dee and her colleague Pat Wilson O'Leary, based on the *Learning Together and Alone* model created by David and Roger Johnson.[1] This skill-oriented method for teaching cooperation is the most successful one we have experienced. By structuring and processing cooperative groups, teachers help students learn about academics, one another, and the social skills necessary to work together productively. In this model cooperative groups differ markedly from traditional groups and are organized around specific teacher expectations of children and groups. Let's take a closer look.

STUDENT INTERACTIONS

The teacher determines the interaction patterns of students within the classroom. Teachers decide how students will interact with materials, the teacher, and one another. Of these three, how students interact with one another gets the least amount of attention from teachers. It also holds the most promise for teaching students cooperative skills.

Teachers can choose from three methods of structuring the student-student interaction within their classrooms: competitive, individualistic, and cooperative.

Competitive Interactions

When the student-student interactions within a classroom are structured competitively, someone wins and everyone else loses. Examples of competitive structuring include spelling bees, reading the most books, rewards for getting done first, and grading on a curve. The outcome in a competitive structure is that if I do well, it hurts your chances of doing well, and if I do poorly, it helps your chances of doing well. The Johnsons state it this way: "If I swim you sink, and if you swim I sink."[2]

Clearly, this structure does little to foster interdependence and cooperation in a classroom. In fact, this structure works against cooperation because it's in the student's self-interest to see classmates do poorly.

We are not suggesting that competition is all bad. If not overdone, it can be energy producing and motivational. It can also spark interest and be a timely change

---

[1]David W. Johnson and Roger T. Johnson, *Learning Together and Alone: Cooperation, Competition, and Individualization* (Englewood Cliffs, NJ: Prentice-Hall, Inc., 1975).

[2] David W. Johnson and Roger T. Johnson, "Cooperative, Competitive, and Individualistic Learning," *Journal of Research and Development in Education* 12, No. 1 (1978), p. 389.

of pace. Used in abundance, however, competitive student interactions work against an Our Classroom feeling.

Individualistic Interactions

The main characteristic of an individualistic structure is that each child faces the learning situation alone. Examples include each student having her own workbook page to complete, reading story to finish, art activity to design, or set of math problems to answer.

With an individualistic goal structure, what one child accomplishes does not affect what any other child accomplishes. Grades or other rewards are in no way tied to how other students in the classroom perform. Each student can earn an A or each student can earn an E. It all depends on what each has accomplished individually.

The individualistic structure defines the student-student interaction so that there is no competition and no interdependence. Students are on their own. There is no incentive to work with or against anyone else. As with a competitive structure, constant emphasis on individualistic tasks undermines efforts to create an Our Classroom feeling.

Cooperative Interactions

A cooperative structuring of the student-student interaction is an effort to build interdependence. Children are arranged in groups, assigned a single product, and then rewarded on the basis of how they do as a group on that product. Everyone in the group gets the same reward. If one child in a group does poorly, it affects the whole group. If one child does well, then that affects the whole group.

The single product in cooperatively structured groups can be creating one mural, completing one math paper, writing one report, or learning one list of spelling words. Individuals within each group are tied together by the emphasis on a single product as well as a shared reward. These rewards are extra recess, lining up first, bonus points, Choice Time minutes, or some other privilege.

Cooperative learning is *not* having students share materials while each individual works on his or her own workbook page. It is *not* having students discuss an assignment together before doing it individually. It is *not* having fast finishers help slow finishers. Cooperative learning as we define and teach it, and as it is practiced in the Johnson model, is much more than students working around a common table, discussing, helping, and sharing materials. The essence of cooperative learning is in assigning a group goal and then rewarding the group together based on the group product.

RATIONALE
FOR TEACHING COOPERATION

Teacher preparation courses have traditionally overlooked the issue of structuring student-student interactions. As a result, teachers have not learned to create intentionally the type of interaction they want among students in their classrooms.

When a teacher is uninformed on structuring student interactions, learning goals are often unclear to both students and teacher. This results in a classroom problem described by Roger Johnson as "fuzzy goal structuring." Students are unclear about whether they are competing, working individually, or working cooperatively. They are also unclear about what behaviors are expected. One student showing another how to do a math problem could be interpreted as cheating or helping depending on the goal structure. Likewise, a student not showing another student how to do a math problem could be interpreted as blocking or helping, depending on the goal structure. Clear goal structures keep students informed on what behaviors are expected of them.

Also traditionally neglected in teacher preparation courses is the whole issue of cooperation. Little time is spent in teacher training institutions helping teachers learn how to deliver cooperative skills to children. More emphasis is placed on competition and individualization. As a result, many teachers know more about individualization and competition than they do about cooperation, and most classrooms reflect that imbalance.

Concern. Of course there's more emphasis in classrooms on individualization and competition than there is on cooperation. The purpose of education is to prepare children for life. The real world is based on competition. Children need to know how to work well alone and better than everyone else to make their mark in our competitive world.

Reply. What we want to see in classrooms is not the elimination of competitive and individualistic goal structures. We want to see a balance, where cooperation is given the same emphasis as the other two. Children need to learn how to work alone so they can rely on themselves and trust their own judgments and individual abilities. They also need to learn about competition so they can compete and accept the outcomes of the challenges they choose. It is just as important, however, that students learn how to enter into interdependent relationships, work together for a common goal, and experience the shared joys of successful cooperation. We want children living and learning about competition, individualization, and cooperation now. Education is more than a preparation for life. Education *is* life.

The days of the rugged individualist are gone. Major contributions to our society don't come from individuals any more. Significant contributions come from institutes—from research teams in which groups of people work cooperatively to advance science, medicine, technology, and other important areas.

Cooperative skills are necessary for high-quality family living as well. The divorce rate would go down if marriage partners were more skilled at getting along. There would be fewer family crises, fewer runaway adolescents, less child abuse, and more positive, loving relationships if family members had more highly developed cooperative skills.

Cooperation, interdependence, and interpersonal skills taught through cooperative groups are appropriate and essential in school, family life, church, the community, business, and government. The skills of cooperation and interdependence are essential if we're going to survive on a planet of finite and dwindling resources. Think about it.

Over 700 studies during the past forty years have explored the issues of competition, cooperation, and individualization. A review of these studies has recently been completed by the Johnsons, which includes several research projects they have conducted.[3] Their conclusions follow.

Competitive Goal Structure

In classrooms where a competitive goal structure is stressed

☆ Students who are different from one another see those differences as threatening
☆ Stereotyping, prejudice, and discrimination increase
☆ Acceptance, understanding, and caring decline

In classrooms where competition is the primary structure, students are continually pitted against one another. Making friends becomes difficult because students spend more time working *against* one another than they do working *with* one another. As a result, trust falls while suspicion rises. In a competitive goal structure, there is simply no incentive to care for others. The message is clear—it's each person for herself.

Individualistic Goal Structure

In classrooms where an individualistic goal structure is stressed

☆ Similarity leads to liking
☆ Stereotyping, prejudice, and discrimination increase
☆ Dissimilarity leads to disliking

[3]David W. Johnson, Roger T. Johnson, and Geoffrey Maruyama, "Interdependence and Interpersonal Attraction between Heterogeneous and Homogeneous Individuals: A Theoretical Formulation, and a Meta-Analysis of the Research." (Submitted for publication, 1982.)

To put it another way, athletes like athletes and dislike their nonathletic classmates. Rural children are more likely to like other rural children and dislike children from the city. Black children tend to like black children. White children tend to like other white children. Boys like boys, girls like girls. Children who dress alike, look alike, act alike, and talk alike like one another. Those who don't, don't.

In individualistically organized classrooms there are few chances for children to work together. As a result of that limitation, children rarely have opportunities to discover the similarities between them and the other students, or to gain an appreciation or understanding of the differences. Because these students don't work together, they seldom get beyond their obvious differences.

Reading and math groups are often the only opportunities that students in individualistically structured classrooms have to work with one another. Because most reading and math groupings are done homogeneously, this usually results in groups of students with similar racial and cultural backgrounds—mixing does not often occur.

Cooperative Goal Structure

In classrooms where a cooperative goal stucture is stressed

☆ Students like the students they cooperate with regardless of differences
☆ Stereotyping, prejudice, and discrimination decrease

Cooperative groups are structured so that students work together to solve problems, learn skills, or produce a group product. Because cooperative group structuring teaches them the skills of working together, children move beyond a surface relationship with one another. Differences are more fully understood and respected. New commonalities are uncovered. Connections are made. Linking occurs.

Students who work in cooperative groups over time learn to like one another. This occurs regardless of their preconceived ideas about differences. As a result, prejudice, stereotyping, and discrimination decrease.

It is clear to us that the research supports our contention that cooperative goal structuring helps teachers create an Our Classroom feeling. Cooperative learning promotes problem solving, togetherness, interdependence, connectedness, self-responsibility, ownership, potency, self-esteem, and self-motivation—all important goals of an Our Classroom environment. As teachers manage their classrooms by structuring in cooperative groups to achieve a balance between competitive and individualistic activities, they strengthen their efforts to create an Our Classroom feeling.

HOW TO ORGANIZE AND TEACH
A COOPERATIVE GROUP LESSON

Facilitating productive cooperative groups doesn't just happen. It takes thorough pre-planning, a tightly structured process, effective communication, and meaningful follow-up. There are important decisions to make ahead of time, strategies for explaining your expectations to children, behaviors to use during group work, and techniques for processing the experience with children. Each is a critical piece in the cooperative learning process. We now offer you a step-by-step explanation of this process.

Issues we will cover are

☆ Group size and makeup
☆ Room arrangement
☆ Content of the lesson
☆ Positive interdependence
☆ Social skills selection and teaching
☆ Monitoring and feedback
☆ How to process group work

Group Size and Makeup

Effective groups consist of anywhere from three to twelve members. Two persons are not enough to generate appropriate social interaction; groups approaching the size of fifteen are so large that few people get to respond. We recommend you begin with three or five participants in each group.

Some other considerations when deciding group size include

Resources. The more people in the group, the greater the group's resources— more brains, more hands, more ideas, more divergent thinking. With fewer people in the group, there are fewer resources available.

Skill level. If students are skilled at working in groups, then a large number will work. If student skills in group work are low, then fewer group members are desirable.

Task size. Generally the larger the task, the more human resources are needed. The smaller the task, the fewer human resources are needed.

Time available. It takes large groups (seven to twelve) more time to reach consensus, finish products, and practice skills. These large groups are effective if there is sufficient time to do the assigned work. Small groups (three to six) are more appropriate if short amounts of time are available. A good rule of thumb is "The shorter the time, the smaller you should make the groups."

Another issue in forming groups is group makeup. For the most part, we recommend heterogeneous groups. Mixed groups in terms of achievement level, sex, race, and interests are desired. Heterogeneous groups bring the best results in terms of high achievement, improved self-esteem, increased acceptance of others, as well as an Our Classroom feeling.

Heterogeneous groups can be assigned by the teacher or organized by random selection. Purposefully separating students who have a past history of not working well together can be helpful at first, especially when you, the teacher, are learning the cooperative group technique. There are also times when it is appropriate to see that at least one strong reader is in each group. The repeated use of teacher-assigned groups, however, sends a message to students that groups have to be formed by the teacher, otherwise they will not succeed. That is not a helpful message to communicate in an Our Classroom environment. Occasionally use randomly selected groups as an alternative to teacher-selected groups. That helps children see that any group can learn to work together cooperatively.

Room Arrangement

Cooperative groups work best with chairs formed in a tight circle. Students sitting face to face, knee to knee, and eyeball to eyeball generate the greatest quantity and quality of interaction. Desks or tables get in the way and tend to put distance (both physical and psychological) between group members. Getting students to work effectively in groups is hard enough without adding physical barriers to the process.

An alternative to unmovable desks is to find another space. Use the library during a free period. If you're stuck in your room, make the best of it. Use two desks with three chairs around them or push desks and tables out of the way.

Content of the Lesson

We suggest beginning with a lesson that covers subject matter well within the success level of your students. The lesson can be learning spelling words, memorizing math facts, writing a story, answering a set of questions about a story, completing a sheet of math problems, or compiling a list of questions about a movie just shown to the entire class. Almost any subject area is appropriate to cooperative group learning as long as the subject matter is not so difficult that a majority of students has trouble with it.

Often teachers use cooperative groups to help students strengthen a skill or concept that has just been taught. For instance, you may teach a total-group lesson on how to multiply and then organize the class into cooperative groups for skill practice and reinforcement of the initial learnings. Or you may ask groups to transfer a concept they just learned in social studies to a mural or poster.

Once you've decided on the content of the lesson, it's time to decide on a specific task for the group to accomplish. Examples of subject matter tasks are

☆ Complete a sheet of ten math problems and know how to explain them.
☆ Learn eight spelling words.
☆ Talk about the movie. Decide and agree on the three main points. Write out a rationale for each main point.
☆ Look through old magazines. Fill the paper with pictures of things that start with the letter *M*.
☆ Practice math facts until everyone knows the seven's, eight's, and nine's.

The task statement describes what you want each group to accomplish. Be sure that you state it specifically, write it out, and put it on display where all the groups can see it.

Positive Interdependence

Positive interdependence is the way groups are tied together. It is the piece of the structure that encourages cooperating by giving students real reasons to work together. Without positive interdependence, group members are less likely to cooperate because there is no reason for them to do so.

It is possible to structure for interdependence in four different ways—reward, accountability, resources, and goal interdependence.

Reward Interdependence. Reward interdependence means that each member of the group shares the same reward. Everyone gets an A or no one gets an A. Everyone gets ten minutes of Choice Time or no one gets ten minutes of Choice Time. Bonus points, stickers, longer recesses, no homework, or healthy treats are other ways to structure positive interdependence into cooperative groups using rewards. Which reward is used is less important than the interdependence achieved by setting it up so that "we sink or swim together."

Reward Interdependence is the strongest and most effective of the four positive interdependence structures. It is especially important while children are first learning how to work in groups. Reward interdependence creates a strong need to work together. We recommend that you use this method during your first few efforts at using cooperative groups. Once students have learned to work effectively in groups, reward interdependence can be replaced with one of the other techniques. The goal is to replace it before students get hooked on it.

Accountability Interdependence. The way the group is held responsible for each individual within the group learning the skill, understanding the process, or mastering the content presented is accountability interdependence. It is not enough in cooperative groups to complete a task together and turn in an acceptable product. Individuals within the group must *all* acquire the knowledge or skill being learned and be able to demonstrate it.

Holding the group accountable for individual members can be achieved in the following three ways:

☆ Have individuals in the group take a test. The average score or the lowest individual score becomes the group score.

☆ Ask one member to explain how the group got a certain answer. If the individual succeeds, the group succeeds. If the individual fails, the group fails.

☆ Randomly select one group member to answer questions about the group's report. Part of the group's reward is based on the selected individual's performance.

Holding groups accountable for each member helps alleviate the problem of one or two bright youngsters doing all the work, commonly found in traditional classroom groups. Too often only one person understands the work and everyone else goes along without understanding. Holding groups accountable for each member encourages isolates to give up that stance. Peer pressure works to get everyone involved because groups never know which member will be asked to explain, demonstrate, or answer questions.

Resource Interdependence. Resource interdependence means that resources are spread around the group. No one member has all the resources, so for the group to complete the task all members must contribute. Resource interdependence can be structured by limiting materials (one ruler or one answer sheet per group). It is also created by dividing up the labor or assigning different roles to each person (one reader, one writer, one dictionary checker).

This style of structuring for interdependence is not as strong as reward interdependence. Having only one pencil or one pair of scissors per group is a reason to work together, but it lacks the strength of a group grade or some other shared reward. We recommend that if you use resource interdependence initially you combine it with reward interdependence.

Goal Interdependence. When a cooperative group shares a common goal, goal interdependence exists. The goal can be to produce a single product (to create a poster or chart), to acquire understanding (to know how to solve a math problem), or to achieve an objective (to reach fifty correct spelling words).

The effectiveness of goal interdependence depends on the level of desire among group members to reach the goal. If achieving the goal is perceived as important, then having a common goal will produce positive interdependence. If the goal is not perceived as important, then little interdependence will be created. Goal interdependence usually becomes more effective after children have had many opportunities to work in groups. Once children experience and understand the excitement, usefulness, and enjoyment of group work, goal interdependence becomes more effective. Until that point is reached, however, we suggest group rewards and accountability to structure interdependence.

Whether you choose reward, accountability, resource, or goal interdependence, positive interdependence is at the heart of cooperative group learning. It is the mechanism that encourages students to work together. It gives them a reason to cooperate. When positive interdependence is in place, students of all ages learn quickly that "we're all in this together." Without positive interdependence there is little incentive for students to work together cooperatively.

Internal Versus External Interdependence. Reward, accountability, and resource interdependence are external techniques. Students want to work together because the situation is structured so that it's in their best interest to cooperate. The reason to work together comes from outside, a structure and organization defined by you, the teacher.

Goal interdependence has an internal focus. It is present when groups feel a strong desire to produce a group product and help one another learn. No external positive interdependence is needed when students achieve this state of motivation. One goal of cooperative learning is to move students increasingly away from external interdependence structures to an internal motivation. Until that ideal is reached, however, reward, accountability, and resource interdependence are more effective.

Social Skills Selection and Teaching

Our Classroom teachers recognize a major advantage in cooperative group learning. They see it as an ideal time to teach students how to work in groups effectively. Working in groups successfully requires specific skills. Unfortunately, children don't often come to school equipped with fully developed group skills. These social skills, as the Johnsons call them, must be taught, practiced, processed, and practiced again before students master them. Cooperative groups are an effective delivery system for teachers who care about children learning cooperative social skills.

Social skills fit into two categories—those necessary to help the group accomplish the task, and those necessary to maintain the group in working order with positive, growing relationships. Both sets of skills are important. Both are assigned, practiced, and processed in cooperative groups.

Task Skills. Task skills help the group move toward completion of the task. They have a content focus and are necessary for groups to get the task done, whether it be a project, report, list, or drawing. Examples of task skills include

☆ Giving ideas
☆ Getting the group back to work
☆ Paraphrasing
☆ Asking questions
☆ Checking others' understanding of the work

These skills help students become effective, on-task, contributing group members who together turn out a high-quality product.

Maintenance Skills. Maintenance skills help the group keep itself in good working order. They have a people focus and help meet the needs of individual group members and strengthen group stability. Examples of maintenance skills are

☆ Encouraging others to talk
☆ Showing acceptance of others
☆ Reducing tension
☆ Acknowledging contributions of others

These skills help students feel better about themselves, one another, and the group.

Both task and maintenance skills are necessary to help groups work effectively. It is not helpful to create groups of students who manage to get the task done, but end up with negative feelings toward one another. Nor is it helpful to create group members who are happy and like one another immensely but seldom acomplish the task. The goal of teaching social skills is to create groups of friendly, on-task students who enjoy their time together, care about one another, and produce high-quality work.

A list of commonly used social skills (compiled by Dee and Pat) follows. Each social skill is described in words appropriate for children in lower-elementary and upper-elementary grades. They are not listed in order of importance.

TASK SOCIAL SKILLS

LOWER ELEMENTARY	*UPPER ELEMENTARY*
Gives ideas	Contributes ideas
Talks about work	Stays on task
Gets group back to work	Directs group work
Looks at others	Makes eye contact
Says back what's been said	Paraphrases
Asks questions	Asks questions
Checks for understanding	Checks for understanding
Stays in seat	Stays in seat

MAINTENANCE SOCIAL SKILLS

LOWER ELEMENTARY	*UPPER ELEMENTARY*
Shares feelings	Shares feelings
Gets others to talk	Encourages others to talk
Responds to ideas	Responds to ideas
Cheerleads	Encourages
Says "Thank you"	Shows appreciation
Uses names	Uses names
Keeps things cool	Relieves tension

Social skills flow from need and are selected on the basis of diagnosis and prescription. If your students show a need for a skill, then use it as the social skill lesson. What skills do your students seem to be lacking? Are they having trouble staying in their seats during group work? If so, that's the place to begin. Do they stay in their seats but not on task? Then select "Stays on task" as the social skill. If your class is heavy into put-downs then "Encourage" is a logical starting point. If many students don't talk during group work then "Encourages others to talk" is appropriate.

Whatever social skill you select, it is important that it be specific. If you diagnose a need not covered on the list provided, examine your choice carefully to make sure your expectations are clear to students. *Listening*, for example, is a skill that teachers often want group members to learn. *Listening*, however, is too general. Break it up into specific behaviors that can be performed and observed. One person talking at a time, acknowledging others' ideas, paraphrasing, and making eye contact are examples of specific behaviors that improve listening.

Cooperating, being helpful, and *being nice* are other examples of behaviors that are not explicit enough to use as social skills. What do you really expect to see and hear when you ask children to be helpful? The more specific you are with your expectations, the greater the chance of getting what you want.

We have found three social skills is the limit that can be successfully practiced at one time. More than three is overload. Two that we recommend for your first few cooperative group lessons are *using names* and *encouraging*. These social skills are powerful in helping group members feel valued and motivated to get the job done. They help groups get off to a successful beginning.

Tips for Teaching Social Skills. Effective cooperative group learning begins with how you choose to see cooperative groups. We suggest you perceive them as mini-labs in which students learn social skills. Like other lab situations, these mini-labs are structured so that students practice the skills, get feedback on them, process the feedback, set goals, and practice more.

The first step in helping children learn any skill is to make sure that they have a clear understanding of what that skill is. With social skills, this step takes place before group work begins. As soon as you have completed sharing your expectations on subject matter with students, introduce social skills.

If "Checks others' understanding of the work" is a social skill you select for the first lesson, don't assume that students know what that means. Begin by naming it and writing "Checks others' understanding of the work" on chart paper. Follow your announcement of the social skill with questions that help students get a clearer understanding of the skill.

☆ What are some ways to check others' understanding of the work?
☆ How do you know when someone is checking your understanding of the work?

☆ What does checking others' understanding look like?

☆ What does checking others' understanding sound like?

Write up student responses on a chart under the headings "Looks like" and "Sounds like."

CHECKS OTHERS' UNDERSTANDING OF THE WORK

SOUNDS LIKE	LOOKS LIKE
"Sam, how do you spell the next word?" "What's 5 × 8, Rhonda?" "Let's all write the words together."	Looks at what's been written. Looks at person reciting. Nods

---

Going through this process helps students realize how serious you are about the importance of social skills. In addition, it helps them get a clearer understanding of the skills. It gives children a list of words and behaviors to use when practicing the skills and it is there if you want to draw attention to it after they work in groups.

Go through the same procedure with each skill the first time it is used. When a skill is being practiced again, simply post the sheet and remind students of the behaviors previously brainstormed and practiced.

Our Classroom teachers know it takes time and effort to teach social skills, and they believe the payoffs are worth the price. They believe that when students learn group skills early in the year, they are able to work successfully in groups throughout the year. Groups that have skills work more successfully and accomplish so many tasks that the initial investment of time, energy, and effort is worth it. In addition, once groups have skills, teachers are able to spend more time working closely with small groups or individuals who can use the attention.

Monitoring and Feedback

Other decisions you need to make before students begin group work are how to monitor students' work on social skills and how to give them feedback on their performance. Students practice social skills while the groups work on the subject matter task. For students to learn from the practice of social skills, feedback must be provided. You need to plan a process to see that this occurs ahead of time.

139

In cooperative groups feedback is collected and shared by an observer who reports on how often group members practice the social skills. Initially we recommend the teacher be the observer. In the beginning students are in the midst of learning the cooperative learning process, which includes several unfamiliar skills. Adding the observer's role and the responsibilities and skills that go with it can be overwhelming when children are becoming familiar with the expectations of group member behavior. Therefore, we recommend the teacher serve as a model by being the observer for several sessions. By the time students are ready to assume that role, they will already be familiar with it, having watched the teacher perform the functions on previous occasions.

Consider using an observation form. It will help you collect information quickly and systematically. The simpler the form, the easier it will be for you to tabulate and share your observations regarding the frequency of social skills used.

SOCIAL SKILLS	SALLY	SARAH	JOHN	MIKE	DWIGHT
_____					
_____					
_____					

Use one form for each group. List the social skills on the left-hand side and place the names of group members across the top. Having these forms completed ahead of time saves time and effort once group work begins. Immediately following your explanation of social skills to students, let them in on what *you* will be doing while they work in groups. Tell them exactly what you are looking for and how you will collect and report the data. Take the mystery out of the observer's role—it reduces student anxiety.

After you have completed all your directions to the class and have shared how you will be observing, group work begins and so does your job as observer. Begin making the rounds from group to group. Sit or stand close enough to groups so that you can see and hear, but not so close that you become a distraction.

Make a tally each time you notice a social skill being used. Obviously you will not notice each time a social skill is practiced. Some will be missed. Remember, you are a human observer and not a videotape machine. The idea here is to collect enough information so that groups get an idea of how often they practice social skills.

When groups have finished working on their tasks, it is important that each individual receive feedback on his or her performance of the skill. Feedback is designed to give students information about their behaviors so they can make conscious decisions about how they want to behave in groups in the future.

When work time is over, give each group its completed observation form. Instruct students to examine the information on the form and discuss it as a group for several minutes.

How to Process Group Work

After you have given the feedback to each group, your role as observer ends and your role as processor begins. This is a critical time in cooperative learning because it is the opportunity for you to help students take a close look at their behaviors and learn from them.

Students learn about groups when they work in groups. They learn even more when they receive objective feedback about how they worked in groups. Learning is increased further when they have time to think about the experience and express their thoughts within the group. Processing helps them do that.

Processing helps group members take a step back to examine their shared experience. It helps individuals take a look at how each performed as a group member and helps the group take a look at how it performed as a unit. Processing groups focuses student thinking and helps students verbally express the experience.

Students evaluate their individual performances in the group by thinking about the feedback that was provided and making a statement about how they view their own behavior. This is accomplished by asking group members to respond to *one* of the following sentence starters:

As a group member I

☆ learned that I . . .
☆ relearned that I . . .
☆ was surprised that I . . .
☆ was happy that I . . .
☆ found that I . . .
☆ was disappointed that I . . .
☆ noticed that I . . .

After you have written one on chart paper, allow for quiet thinking time. Then have students individually write out a response. A written response increases the likelihood that they will have something unique to share out loud later. When groups are ready, students share what they have written. Group members do not respond verbally to the sharing. They simply listen, letting each member have a turn without commenting.

Notice that the emphasis in the sentence starters is on *I*. This is done to help group members focus on how *they* did individually rather than on how others did. Students are encouraged to do self-examination and to own their feelings and thoughts. It further helps to eliminate blaming others for group failures.

You can also structure the processing so students give positive feedback to one another, which is necessary for them to evaluate their own performance. Structure this activity tightly so that student comments are confined to social skill behavior only. Set it up so their comments begin with one of the following.

_____, I appreciated it when you . . .
    (name)

_____, I liked it when you . . .

_____, I enjoyed it when you . . .

_____, I admired the way you . . .

Direct the student giving the statement to look at the person she is speaking to and use his name when sharing. Have the person who receives the positive feedback maintain eye contact and say "Thank you" or remain silent. This structuring must be carefully explained and monitored. Giving and receiving positive feedback in our culture is not a skill that is valued or fully developed. Children are more accustomed to giving each other put-downs than they are to giving positive feedback. Yet with proper structure and a serious attitude, this skill can be learned and used effectively.

The group as a whole can also evaluate its performance with a variety of methods, some of which follow.

Group Discussions. Use one or more of the following questions to stimulate thinking and verbal sharing.

☆ How well did we do on each of the social skills?
☆ Which social skill did we do the best job on?
☆ Which social skill could we do better on next time?

Once groups have had a chance to discuss this issue, have a spokesperson from each group report the group findings. Record responses on chart paper for all to see.

Continuums. A continuum is a line with an extreme at each end.

NEVER_____ALWAYS

Students place an *X* on the line in a spot that best represents what actually happened in their group. Examples follow.

Everyone talked in our group.	NEVER	_____ALWAYS
More that one person directed the group's work.	NEVER	_____ALWAYS
Each person was encouraged in our group.	NEVER	_____ALWAYS

Group members individually mark the continuums and then compare with other group members' opinions. Discussion follows.

Open-Ended Questions. Process questions are more effective if they are open ended. The open-ended question "How was it for you to use names today?" will produce more dialogue than the close-ended "Did you use names today?" Close-ended questions ("Did you feel encouraged today?") will produce little more than "Yes" and "No" answers. Open-ended questions ("Tell how encouraged you felt today") will help you avoid having constantly to ask "Why?" to the "Yes" and "No" responses.

Goal Setting. Goal setting is the link between how groups did today and how they will do tomorrow. It is the vehicle that moves groups from a collection of unskilled individuals to a tightly knit, skilled unit.

One way to structure goal setting is to ask groups to discuss and reach consensus on a one-sentence completion. "Our group could do better on social skills by . . ." or "One thing we'd do differently next time is. . . ." Group responses are then written on a large sheet of chart paper headed "Our Group Goals."

Individual goal setting can be handled in the same way. Students individually respond to the sentence starter "Something I will do differently next time is. . . ." Individual and group goal statements can then be recorded in a group folder for review before the next cooperative group lesson. When groups reconvene for the next lesson, the goals in the folder remind students of what to work on during that session.

The importance of processing the group work cannot be overemphasized. It is the piece most often left out by teachers or tabled until the following day. Our Classroom teachers recognize the value of processing and plan ten minutes in each session for that purpose. They don't compromise when it comes to processing, for they realize this procedure helps students reflect on and integrate learnings from one group experience to the next.

DIFFERENCES BETWEEN
TYPICAL CLASSROOM GROUPS
AND COOPERATIVE GROUPS

The differences between cooperative and typical classroom groups are not always apparent to educators untrained in the specifics of cooperative learning. Yet differences exist from preplanning to processing. To help draw a clear distinction between cooperative groups and typical classroom groups we will examine several issues.

Leadership

Typical classroom groups usually have one leader. That leader, whether chosen by the teacher or the group, is often the best reader, the most popular person, or the most assertive group member. Leadership rarely changes, and power struggles are frequent.

Leadership in a cooperative group is divided into specific behaviors—social skills. The assumption is that all students can learn these behaviors, so all members are invited to perform and practice them. Leadership is distributed around the group with everyone leading from time to time. Whatever is needed in the way of leadership can be done by any group member. Everyone is responsible to see that leadership exists.

Group Makeup

A characteristic of classroom groups as they are typically organized is homogeneity. Reading groups, math groups, and special-interest groups tend to clump students who are most alike together. Students don't often get opportunities to work with others of different abilities or interests.

Heterogeneity is the objective of cooperative groups. Groups are more often dissimilar, with members of each sex, race, interest level, and ability level divided among them.

Success

The success of the individual is unrelated to that of other group members in typical classroom groups. What one member does has no effect on the others. There is no interdependence, so members have little incentive to cooperate.

In the cooperative group structure the success of an individual is related to the success of all the others in the group. Because of the built-in positive interdependence, students are tied together with reward, resources, or accountability. The concept "We sink or swim together" is created intentionally.

Products

Group members in typical classroom groups generally create individual products. Each person turns in her own paper, report, map, or story.

In cooperative groups the emphasis is on a single product from the group. Only one paper, one report, one map, or one story is produced.

Rewards

Rewards in typical classroom groups are passed out individually. Members turn in individual products, and they are rewarded on the basis of those products.

A shared reward is characteristic of cooperative groups. What one group member receives as a reward all group members receive.

Social Skills

In typical classroom groups teachers generally tell students to "Get along" or "Cooperate." Little time is spent on instruction, skill practice, or discussion of what is meant by cooperation. Children are expected to cooperate and often don't have the skills necessary to meet that expectation.

Social skills are an integral part of cooperative groups. They occupy a place of equal importance with subject matter. Time, effort, and attention are given to social skill explanation, practice, feedback, and processing. Teachers believe skilled group members are made, not born, and their actions reflect that belief.

Teacher's Behavior

Teachers who organize typical classroom groups generally behave as *interventionists*. Interventionists believe that students need them to point out when and where they are acting appropriately and inappropriately. These teachers expect to set the standards of effective behavior and believe that they are needed to enforce those behaviors. They rescue individuals and groups.

Behaviors of interventionists include

1. Breaking into groups to offer solutions when there seems to be a problem
2. Answering questions from individuals during observation time
3. Listening to students complain about other group members
4. Giving advice to individuals or groups
5. Repeating instructions upon request
6. Telling groups to "Get back to work," "Stop that," "Be quiet," and so forth

Teachers who organize cooperative groups generally behave as *interactionists*. Interactionists believe that students learn appropriate and inappropriate behavior by encountering others and being confronted with feedback on their behavior. They believe standards of behavior evolve from students learning to accommodate others while others are learning to accommodate them. Interactionists trust the structure and the process of cooperative learning. They believe that within each group enough resources already exist to solve any problem. They do not rescue, but instead turn problems back to the group for discussion and solution.

Behaviors of interactionists include

1. Informing students that the teacher will not be available during observation time to solve problems, and that groups will have to work things out themselves

2. Stepping in only if the group as a whole decides to ask for help and checking that out before giving assistance

3. Continuing to turn problems back to the group by asking questions like "What have you done so far to correct this problem?"

4. Not interacting with or interrupting the group during observation time

5. Not repeating instructions but replying instead, "Someone in your group knows"

6. Allowing groups to struggle and make mistakes

7. Interrupting only if a serious problem develops and saying, "Excuse me, I'm interrupting your group," followed by descriptive feedback on the situation. Groups are then expected to solve the problem

Typically interventionists work to solve students' problems or even prevent problems from occurring. Interactionists work to help students solve their own problems. Simply, interventionists *intervene* and interactionists *interact*.

In this chapter we have detailed the difference between cooperative and traditional classroom groups while sharing a model for conducting your own cooperative groups. We hope you now realize more than ever that cooperation in classrooms doesn't just happen. It must be structured in, managed, and processed. Cooperative group learning is a model to help you do that. It is a structure that provides continuity and direction as you plan and facilitate cooperative behaviors in your classroom.

Humanness

10

we begins with me

The focus of this book up to now has been on creating an Our Classroom feeling by building within a classroom group feelings of togetherness, interrelatedness, and cooperation. So far we have concentrated on the total group and have suggested ways to strengthen feelings of us, we, our. We have shared thoughts on building ownership and sharing control, ideas for creating unity and rootedness, and strategies for inviting cooperation and responsibility. We have suggested that to create an Our Classroom feeling teachers need to spend time, effort, and energy building group pride, structuring group work, and establishing group goals. All that is true. Yet, in another sense, *we* begins with *me*.

☆ Individuals who don't like themselves have trouble liking others.

☆ Individuals with little self-respect experience trouble respecting others.

☆ Individuals uncommitted to personal goals have trouble committing to group goals.

☆ Individuals with little self-confidence have trouble generating confidence in the group.

☆ Individuals who feel impotent have trouble experiencing the potency of the group.

This chapter is about strengthening *we* by strengthening *me*. In it you will learn strategies for helping students become aware of their existing self-images and explore ways to invite them to strengthen those images. You will learn the skills necessary to create an environment that enhances individual self-esteem as well as techniques to help children feel more potent.

To begin this chapter we'd like to have you do the following exercise.[1] Find a quiet comfortable place to sit, one where you will be undisturbed for several minutes. Read the entire exercise through before you begin.

Close your eyes. Begin to relax. Let all the tension flow from your body. Concentrate on your breathing. Breathe deeply using your abdomen. Notice where one breath starts and another stops. Breathe more deeply. Feel the tension leaving your body on each out breath. Enjoy this activity as you relax into it.

Now hold out your hand and imagine you are holding an apple. Still keeping your eyes closed, examine your apple. Look it over. What do you notice? What color is your apple? Does it have spots or blemishes on it? Is it heavy or light? Is it smooth, rough, or some combination of the two? Spend a minute or two getting to know your apple. What is its shape? Does it have a name? What do you like about it? Notice any uniqueness that exists.

Now using your imagination, trade apples with me. Give me yours and take mine. Examine my apple for a minute or two. Compare it with the one you had before, while I examine your apple.

Now trade back and reacquire your original apple. Examine it again for a few sec-

[1]Adapted from Dov Peretz Elkins, *Teaching People to Love Themselves*, rev. ed. (Rochester, NY: Growth Associates, 1978), pp. 87–88.

onds and then open your eyes. (Now complete the entire exercise before you go on. Do it now!)

☆   How did you feel about your apple as compared with mine? Which was better?

☆   Did you experience any sense of relief when you got your original apple back?

☆   Did you have any difficulty changing the image from your apple to mine? Did you experience any difficulty changing the image back?

☆   Can you still visualize your apple? Can you close your eyes and see it? Can you see it with your eyes open?

THE IMPORTANCE OF IMAGES

If you are like the hundreds of participants who have done this exercise at one of our workshops, you probably had little trouble creating an image of an apple. In fact, participants often report becoming strongly attached to their apples, images that they created in a second and became extremely familiar with in sixty to ninety seconds. Some participants also share that they find it difficult to let go of the apple image they created for themselves. Some people can still see the image hours and even days later.

How about you? Can you still see the apple you created for yourself? Do you think you'll be able to see it tomorrow? Next week?

Now compare the apple image with the image you have of yourself. If an image of an apple, which you created in ninety seconds, is difficult to forget and to change, imagine how difficult it is to change an image that you've worked a lifetime to create!

I have been working on my self-image for over forty years. I have a lot of time and effort invested in it. I'm not going to change it whimsically or quickly. My self-image evolves slowly and is not easily changed. How about you? How easily is your self-image altered? Think about it.

Students in your classroom also bring with them a lifetime of image building. By the time students arrive in your classroom, they have already accumulated several years of experiences that have created and cemented their own unique self-images. For them, too, the self-image will not be easily altered.

The students who come to us, whether we teach kindergarten or work with sixth graders, come with a variety of self-images that range from confidence and *I Can-ness* on one extreme to self-loathing and *I Can't-ness* on the other.

Our job as educators is to nurture and support those students who have healthy, positive self-images, while at the same time helping students with low self-images to see themselves as more worthwhile, more able, and increasingly capable. It is not an easy task.

We believe people tend to act in ways that are consistent with their self-images. Simply put, if a child sees herself as a troublemaker, she makes trouble. If a child sees herself as a leader, she leads. If a child sees herself as able, she acts able.

When students, other adults, or we ourselves act in accordance with our self-images, it feels good. That consistency feels comfortable. Acting in line with our self-image tends to generate within us that comfortable "at-home" feeling. Similarly, acting in ways not consistent with our perception of ourselves tends to feel uncomfortable.

Once a self-image is created, it is not easily changed. We emphasize that point not to dissuade you from trying to help students move toward healthier perceptions of themselves, but rather to remind you of how critically important it is to create an environment that helps students develop positive self-images in the first place.

Because a child acts in accordance with his self-image, the formation of that image is critical. And while your students have already formed the perceptions they have of themselves, they are also in the process of reforming those images.

A self-image is not a totally rigid, unalterable picture. It is modified by every life experience and the interpretations we attach to those experiences. It is built and altered slowly, over time, through an accumulation of our life events and contacts with others. Teachers have daily opportunities to add to that accumulation and interpretation of experiences for every youngster in their classrooms.

Teachers can affect the self-images of students in two ways. The first is by creating an environment of acceptance and support where high self-esteem can develop. The second is by designing activities, materials, and processes that lead children to an ever-increasing awareness of themselves and their self-images. As a student gets a clearer picture of what his self-image is, he is in a better position to judge for himself if that's the image he wants. He can then move in the direction of creating a useful, positive image of himself in line with his own desires. Teachers create the atmosphere necessary to nourish or diminish self-esteem and the growth of positive or negative self-images.

Teachers have a tremendous impact on how children see themselves. Their choice of words, voice tone, nonverbal clues, and general attitude toward children have impact. The arrangement of the classroom, the emphasis on competitiveness or cooperation, the rewards and consequences, and the structuring of interaction patterns play a part. The design of activities, the determination of appropriate success levels, and the style of school-to-home communications have a role in determining how children choose to see themselves. In fact, almost everything teachers do, consciously or unconsciously, affects the way children perceive themselves.

We believe that teachers who create the most supportive, nourishing climates for the development of high self-esteem do so on purpose. Again, the issue is intentionality. Our Classroom teachers want supportive, nourishing climates. They plan for them. They structure them in. And they create them.

Our Classroom teachers design activities and areas of the classroom where children come to see themselves as able. We call them "I Can" places and activities. These "I Can" places are at the heart of an Our Classroom environment and are designed to foster high self-esteem.

An "I Can" place is an area in the classroom where teachers celebrate the things that children can do. It's a place specifically designed to showcase successes, to highlight strengths, and to give visibility to self-worth.

We recommend that you plaster classrooms, doors, hallways, the principal's office, or any other available space with areas that shout "I can!" Following are some ways to do that.

JOURNALS

Begin "I Can" journals. Have students develop a permanent record of things that they can do. Encourage them to share entries during Sharing Time. Share some of yours.

PROUD CHAIN

Create a Proud Chain. Students write statements about things they are proud of on strips of paper. The first one is pasted together to form a circle and is hung from the ceiling. Links to the chain are added as children and teachers think of new things they're proud of.

WORD RINGS

Word rings are effective with children who are just learning to read. As a child masters a new word she puts it on a card and carries it on a ring attached to her clothing (belt loops are useful here). The child reads the ring of cards to people throughout the day, who in turn sign the last card. I observed a child in one first-grade classroom whose belt loop contained the signatures of four teachers, a custodian, two cooks, one bus driver, two parents, one grandparent, a principal, and thirteen other children. What validation!

THINGS OUR HANDS CAN DO

Title a bulletin board "Things Our Hands Can Do." Students and teacher trace around their own hands, cut out the silhouettes, and fill them with appropriate statements. Some possibilities are

- ☆ My hands can draw things
- ☆ My hands can do math
- ☆ My hands can bake cookies
- ☆ I can write with my hands

"I CAN" CAN

Create an "I Can" can. Get a small can and fill it with open-ended "I Can" statements.

- ☆ One great thing that *I can* do with my mind is . . .
- ☆ One great thing that *I can* do with my body is . . .
- ☆ Things that *I can* do now that I couldn't one year ago are . . .
- ☆ Things *I can* do on the playground are . . .
- ☆ Something that I'm good at on the weekend is . . .

On a file card have students copy and complete each statement. They then add them to a giant "I Can" can that sits in a prominent place in the classroom.

PROUD LINE

Stretch a clothesline or wire across the room. Use it to let students display things that they *can* do. Display something of yours.

BEST BOARDS

Section off a wall into thirty one-foot portions using tape. Each student chooses a space and puts his name on it. That space becomes his own private Best Board. Students use Best Boards to show off their best work. Three rules are helpful.

1. Something must always be in the space.
2. It must be changed at least once a week.
3. Each person decides what goes in his or her space.

Don't forget to provide a space for yourself.

CAPABLE KITES

Students design Capable Kites out of construction paper in the shape of diamonds. A photo or self-portrait plus the student's name is added to the body of the kite. Students list things they are capable of on the tail.
Examples include

☆ Running around the entire playground without stopping
☆ Being kind and friendly
☆ Hitting a ball fifty feet
☆ Reading a hundred-page book in two days

WHEN I WAS/NOW I AM BOOKS

Students make individual books using the theme "When I Was/Now I Am."

When I was three I couldn't _____ , but now that I am nine I can _____ .

Each page contains a similar statement with a different year and a drawing to go with it.

BRIGHT IDEAS

Have children make paper light bulbs. On the front of each bulb they write a bright idea they have had.

SUCCESS OBJECTS

Success objects are materials created in school or brought from home that are tangible proof that a person has had a success. Examples include trophies, awards, ribbons, certificates, photographs, and newspaper articles.

Have students bring a success object from home that reveals some of their successfulness. Objects can be something they made (model airplane), won (third place in horseback riding), or had presented to them (certificate for being a successful newspaper carrier). Children then share orally about their success objects, telling how they got them, how they felt, and anything else they would like to add.

As an alternative have students design their own success objects. One teacher, piggybacking on student interest in the winter Olympics, had students design gold medals for themselves. Students were asked to identify something they were good at in winter. Gold medals that students designed for themselves included figure skating, skiing, sledding, shoveling snow, throwing snowballs, and sitting indoors reading books.

PHOTO BOOKS

Use your camera to record major accomplishments like

☆ Walter sharing with Bill his new Level 4 reading book
☆ Jenny completing her twentieth push-up
☆ Jake holding up his math paper revealing a perfect effort of eights and nines

FIRSTS

Create a class book entitled "Firsts." Students are encouraged to add a page to it any time that they complete a first in their lives.

☆ I rode my bike for the *first* time.
☆ This is my *first* trip to Florida.
☆ I got all the spelling words right for the *first* time.
☆ I lost my *first* tooth.

Firsts are motivational. They are proof that our risks are worth it. They expand our awareness of living and increase both our understanding and appreciation of growth and change. They are benchmarks in our lives.

What positive impact you have if you create a classroom environment where firsts can take place and are celebrated. Why not start here *first*?

CAREER BOOKS

"I Can" career books are useful for helping students at an early age develop pictures of themselves as able to take part in many careers. Each page contains a picture representing a job that the child believes she could do, along with a two- or three-sentence explanation.

☆ I can be a doctor. She takes care of her patients and makes them well.

☆ I can be a lawyer. She helps people in trouble.

☆ I can be a skydiver. She doesn't get scared and has lots of fun.

TEACHERS' LOUNGE

How about an "I Can" place for your teachers' lounge? What can you create there that will help showcase teacher successes or highlight the strengths of your colleagues? How about making Capable Kites at your next staff meeting? Or "I Can" chains? Or why not begin a Best Board or Proud Wall? Think about it.

CHILDREN'S EFFORTS ON DISPLAY

"I Can" places are one way Our Classroom teachers help children see their able-ness, their capable-ness, and their responsible-ness. Displaying students' efforts is another technique for helping them perceive their strengths and capabilities.

We watched one kindergarten teacher walk around all morning wearing a roll of masking tape like a bracelet. We noticed that she used it frequently to help children display their work. Whenever a youngster finished a paper, she was on the spot with pieces of tape. Posting the paper on a nearby wall always followed.

Not all Our Classroom teachers wear masking tape bracelets. Yet most of them value displaying children's efforts. We communicate a lot to children about how we value their efforts by what we do with them. If we let them fold up everything, stick it in their back pockets, and take it home, never to be seen again, we have communicated something about how we value their work without saying a word. On the other hand, if we take some of our time and effort to make creative displays that showcase their work, we have told children something else about how we value their efforts. And we still haven't said a word.

Our Classroom teachers teach children to display their own work. They invite children to label their creations with titles and proudly display their names, because names signal recognition. Anyone in Our Classroom who works long and hard deserves recognition. It's more proof that *I can.*

Take a mental trip to your own classroom now. Look around. What do you see on the walls? Are your walls bare or do you have children's work on display? Is there some contribution from every child there? Does the room have the flavor of children or is it filled with purchases from your local teachers' store? Think about it.

When children sit in the middle of the classroom, look around, and see a piece of their artwork, they see proof of their importance. If they see red, green, and blue objects they found outside during the recent Color Walk, they see proof of their existence. Putting students' contributions in visible places lends proof of their importance in our shared environment. They feel more strongly that this is "our" classroom.

Begin today to generate more space to showcase "I Can-ness." Use the back of the piano, bookcase, or filing cabinet. Use the hall, the cafeteria, or the principal's office. Ask your custodian for her opinions on how you can add display space.

☆ Stretch two wires across the classroom. Use clothespins to hold student papers.

☆ Gather old picture frames. Display students' art and writing. Change frequently.

☆ Buy a fishnet. Hang it from the ceiling. Display students' work on both sides.

☆ Remove the commercial bulletin boards. Put children on display, not merchandise!

☆ Use staples, tape, tacks, pins, string, and anything else you can think of. Get children's work out where they can see it!

"I CAN" TIME

A few years ago when we first began collecting Our Classroom ideas, Judy Risdon and Liz Murphy team-taught a group of fifty second and third graders. On one occasion, I walked into their shared classroom after lunch to find children in turn, performing somersaults, standing on their heads, and crab walking across the floor. An audience of peers sat on the sidelines watching.

The scene resembled a cross between a gym class and a circus. It was neither. The second and third graders at this school were simply starting the afternoon with "I Can" Time.

"I Can" Time was a space during the day where children and teachers celebrated the things that they *could do*. There was no set time, no list of participants, no requirements. "I Can" Time occurred at any time during the day that seemed appropriate. This day it happened after lunch.

The activity began when Judy suggested to one child that she share some things she had been learning in gymnastics. The child agreed to perform one trick. Children who had returned from lunch watched as some fancy-named flip was executed. Those who watched displayed their appreciation by applauding.

Another child volunteered to share what she could do. Soon the process of sharing was in full gear. As children returned to the room, they caught the spirit and chose to join either the audience or the growing number of volunteers.

Liz, the other member of this teaching team, came upon the scene in the same way that many of the children did. She returned from lunch to find Jason standing on his head. Liz first joined the excitement as a member of the audience. Then she chose to risk.

Her effort was some sort of flip. Form, poise, and execution notwithstanding, the children loved it. A teacher had chosen to share a part of herself, to reveal a bit more of her humanness. They were delighted.

The end of the activity came naturally. As interest and enthusiasm burned itself out, the sharing ended. Children and teachers simply turned their attention to other parts of their day. One by one they scattered throughout the two rooms pursuing new interests. "I Can" Time had ended as naturally as it had begun.

"I Can" Time doesn't have to be acrobatics. It can involve reading or math or art. It can be a celebration of writing or speaking or acting. What it involves matters less than that it happens.

How can you use "I Can" Time in your situation? How can you adapt this idea to help you help children perceive their "I Can-ness"? *Where* and *when* and *how* will you organize an "I Can" Time? Write it out now. Set a goal for yourself. Yes, you can!

THE LANGUAGE OF "I CAN"

Language plays an important role in determining whether children develop an "I Can" or an "I Can't" consciousness. Children, and adults as well, limit themselves daily and sabotage their own self-esteem by choosing unhelpful, un-self-responsible language. Teachers concerned with helping students develop "I Can" behaviors help them to appreciate the significance of their everyday language and the influence that language has on their lives.

One step necessary for teaching children to choose less limiting language is to work with them on becoming aware of their own chosen words and teach them how to monitor those words. A good way for teachers to begin to do that is to start with paying attention to their *own* choice of language. Consider the following exercise, which we learned from our friend Tim Timmermann.

Please do the following language activity. It is important that you *do* this entire activity instead of just reading about it.

Complete the following sentence starter: "I can't. . . ." Write five responses to it, finishing it with statements that are true for you. Your replies can be professional.

☆ I can't get kids to behave.
☆ I can't stand my principal.

Or your responses can be personal.

☆ I can't lose ten pounds.
☆ I can't quit smoking.

Write yours now. (If you can't think of any, that can be your first one.)

When you have completed five or more endings to the sentence starter, read them silently and then read them again, out loud, with emotion. Pay attention to how the words sound and what you feel as you read them.

As the next step in this exercise, go back through the statements and cross out the word *can't*. Replace it with *don't*. Now you have the same statements with the words "I don't" heading them.

Read these silently and out loud. Pay attention to how they sound. Notice if your statements have changed in any way. Notice if you feel any differently about them. When you have finished, write your reactions starting with the words below.

☆ I noticed . . .
☆ I learned . . .
☆ I relearned . . .
☆ I believe . . .

Now cross out the word *don't* and replace it with *won't*. Again, read your statements silently and then out loud, focusing on whether or not the word change alters your statements in any way. Also monitor your feelings. When you have finished, again write your reactions.

☆ I noticed . . .
☆ I felt . . .
☆ I wonder . . .

Now replace *won't* with the phrase "choose not to." One more time monitor your thoughts and feelings as you notice your statements. Pay attention to what happens to them. Now record your reactions.

☆ I feel . . .
☆ I learned . . .
☆ I believe . . .

We wish we could hear how you experienced this exercise. We're wondering if you had reactions similar to those of others who have attended our workshops. They comment

☆ I felt guilty when I used *don't*.
☆ *Don't* made me feel more responsible.
☆ *Won't* seemed too final.
☆ I felt more in control with *don't* and *won't*.
☆ I *can't* feels more comfortable.
☆ I *don't* like admitting that I'm choosing not to quit smoking.

We get a variety of reactions to this activity. Participants' comments reflect many different beliefs and values. Their reactions indicate several ways to experience this exercise.

The interpretation that we attach to the "can't/don't/won't/choose not to" language is this: "I can'ts" are almost always lies. At best, they are untruths.

Saying "I can't" is a way of giving up responsibility, a way of disowning our place in the decision-making process. It is a choice of words that helps us see situations as not under our control. It helps us be non-self-directing and play victim. Saying "I can't" is not only unhelpful, it is also an inaccurate description.

☆ While most "I can'ts" are lies, it is true that some are real.

☆ *I can't* jump over a building without the aid of some apparatus.

☆ *I can't* grow another foot taller.

☆ *I* (Chick) *can't* bear children.

Yet most of the "I can'ts" that we hear ourselves saying are not true.

☆ I can't come over now. (I'm choosing to do something else.)

☆ I can't play the piano. (I've chosen to spend the time in my life learning other things.)

☆ I can't keep a secret. (I choose not to keep a secret.)

One woman challenged us in a workshop saying, "I have one 'I can't' that's real. I can't visit my children very often." Chick asked her to explain. She replied, "They live in California and it's too expensive to travel there." He then asked if she owned her own home, to which she responded that she did.

"Sell it," he suggested, "move into an apartment and you'll have enough money to see your children every weekend."

"I could do that," she said, "but I'm not going to make that choice." Her last word was the one that revealed the real issue. Most of our "I can'ts" are simply decisions we make and priorities we choose. Yes, they are choices.

I want to be more consistent in my life using language that leaves me in a place that I like. "I can't" language leaves me in a place I don't like, a place of self-evaluation that rates me as a person who *can't*. I find it more useful to describe myself as a person who can, but for any number of legitimate reasons chooses not to right now.

☆ I can learn to downhill ski. I just don't want to devote the necessary time and effort to that right now.

☆ I can spell well if I take the time to learn. It's just not important to me at this point in my life.

Whenever I hear myself saying "I can't" I want to use the other words (don't, won't, choose not to) instead, to see what I'm really telling myself. Sometimes I mean *I don't*

(I don't run 10,000 meters in under forty minutes yet). Other times I mean *I won't* (I won't enjoy heights). And sometimes I mean *I choose not to* (I choose not to sleep in on weekends).

Do you have children in your classrooms who say "I can't"? We bet that you do, and our hunch is that you're tired of hearing them say it! The words have a whiny ring to them.

☆ I *can't* figure it out.
☆ I *can't* get my gloves on.
☆ I *can't* find any.
☆ I *can't* think of one.

That choice of language is destructive to children. It's a way for them to dodge responsibility, to disown, and not to accept themselves as being in charge of their own lives. It also helps program their subconscious minds with negatives.

When you hear children using "I can't," ask them to change their words. When our son Matt comes to us and says, "I can't get my snowmobile suit zipped up," we suggest that he change his words. We ask him to say "don't" instead of "can't." When he says, "I don't get my snowmobile suit zipped up," we simply thank him and let it go at that. After three or four similar encounters, he has figured it out. Now he seldom says "I can't" and usually catches himself when he does.

Helping children learn new words to say in place of *can't* is important. It is more helpful for them to describe their behavior with *don't, won't* or *choose not to* than to evaluate it with *can't*. The word change assists them to see themselves as people who *haven't yet*, rather than as people who *can't*.

One teacher we observed got so tired of students saying "I can't" that she made a giant tombstone from construction paper, wrote "I Can't" and "R.I.P." on it, then displayed it. She explained to students that "I Can't" was dead and was never to be heard from again. Whenever the word surfaced, she pointed to the tombstone. Children got the message.

What is your typical response to students who say "I can't"? We used to say, "Come on, try." It wasn't until recently that we discovered *trying* doesn't work. Trying is a cop-out. Anyone who is busy trying is not busy doing. Trying doesn't work. *Doing* does.

To help children do, rather than try, teach them to "act as if." "I can't" is a block and is usually accompanied by thoughts of self-doubt, self-consciousness, or self-deprecation. "Acting as if," or pretending, is a way of giving the mind something else to do rather than self-doubting. If the mind is busy "acting as if," it's too busy to be doubting itself.

Think about any new challenge in your life. Maybe you're learning to ride a motorcycle, plant a garden, or play a musical instrument. When do you know for sure, beyond all doubt, that you can do it? Not until you *do* it. You really don't know for sure if you can do it until you *do* it.

We believe that everything you do from the time you decide to learn something new until you actually accomplish it is an act. Because you don't know if you can do it or not, you act. You can choose to act as if you can or you can choose to act as if you can't.

Some of you are teaching new grade levels this year. Perhaps you never taught second grade before. You don't know if you can do it or not. You think you can but you don't know for sure. And you won't know until you actually do it. Our hunch is that you'll face that assignment "acting as if" you can. If you "act as if" you can't, you won't be there very long.

There are many children in our classrooms doing an "I can't" act. And it is an act, an act that they have chosen, whether they are aware of their choice or not. We believe that it's time we started calling children on their acts. It's time for some of them to start choosing other acts.

Getting students to "act as if" is one way to help them change their acts. By having them "pretend" from time to time, it is more likely that they will see the choices they have. They will learn eventually that they are the ones who turn the act on and off. They push the control button.

Another way to help children become increasingly aware that they are at the controls is consistently to use words and actions that communicate to them that you know it's their act.

☆ Martha, I see you *choosing* to be a slow starter today.

☆ Robert, you're *I can't–ing* again. I'd like you to change your act.

☆ I see that you have *decided* to be friendly this morning, Tyrone. Why are you *choosing* that?

☆ Jessie, the noise is affecting my concentration. Would you find a different way to *act*, please?

The more we communicate to children that we understand that they choose their own act, the harder it becomes for them to deny their place in that choice. The more they see and believe they control their own acts, the more aware of their own power they become and the more often they will choose acts that are self-enhancing and useful.

POSITIVE PICTURING

Positive picturing is another powerful tool for helping children develop an "I can" consciousness. Positive picturing is using the imagination to picture the positive process and outcome of an upcoming activity. It is practicing the activity in the mind, a sort of mental run-through of the performance or expected outcome.

One significant element related to achievement is the ability to visualize whatever you want to achieve. If you're not able to see yourself doing it, chances are that you won't do it well.

In schools

☆ Children won't act properly in the halls unless they have a picture in their minds of what acting properly actually is.

☆ Children won't read smoothly without interruptions unless they have a picture and a belief of themselves doing just that.

☆ Children will not exercise alternatives to fighting unless they can visualize those alternatives. Without pictures in their minds of what those alternatives look like, how can students possibly choose them? They are not response-able.

☆ You will very likely not become an administrator if you cannot "see" yourself doing administrative behaviors and doing them successfully.

☆ You will not enjoy teaching unless you have pictures in your mind of teaching being an exciting, challenging, rewarding profession. If you carry negative pictures about teaching around with you, chances are you are a negative teacher.

Practicing something in your head can be as effective as physical practice. Athletes and other performers have used this technique for years. In addition to sports, visualization has been used in medicine and healing, romance, business, politics, and many other facets of life. The tool of repetitious positive picturing is a strong agent in helping people achieve their goals. The ability to visualize what you want is one of the tools necessary to get it. The technique has tremendous potential for education and improving the learning process.

Using children's imaginations to put positive pictures in their minds is one way to help them change the way they see themselves. As we have stated before, a child won't act successful until she begins to see herself as successful.

Doug Levine, a Houston, Texas, teacher, uses positive picturing to help seventh graders follow directions. According to Doug,

> Repeating directions usually meets with blank stares, so I ask my students to picture in their minds what their papers will look like when they are finished—how many sentences there will be or the arrangement of answers. I also ask them to picture what they will do with their papers and themselves after they finish. I ask them to get in touch with what they will feel like when they are finished and to picture how they will answer for themselves the question of what to do next.

Doug liked the results. He contends,

When I go through this routine with them it works 100 percent of the time. When I don't, a dozen students ask me what page we're on, where to put their papers, and what to do when they're finished.

Having children visualize the successful outcome of following directions is helping Doug get what he wants from children. In addition, the picturing helps them see themselves as able.

Other examples of positive picturing follow.

THE ASSEMBLY

OK, Class, put your heads down now and relax. Breathe deeply. Count your breaths. Take slow, deep breaths. Get a rhythm going. While you are concentrating on your breathing, imagine a giant TV screen in your head. I am going to ask you to see some pictures there. Notice yourself walking down the hall with our class to the assembly. See how orderly and quietly we walk as a class. Other people are noticing. Watch them watch us. Feel proud and smile to yourself. See yourself enjoying the assembly and applauding at the end. Watch as we are dismissed. Again, see the quiet exit and flow of our class as we walk back to our room. See yourself sitting in the room, alert and ready for the remainder of the morning. Feel good about our passage in the hall. Feel alive and full of energy as you see yourself sitting at your desk. When you are ready, open your eyes and rejoin us. (Pause) Now let's line up for the assembly.

This visualization lets children know what you expect. It puts positive pictures of the desired behavior in their minds. It gives them the opportunity to see themselves doing what you expect and to experience positive feelings about it. It doesn't matter that the experience was imagined. What children can imagine and hold in their minds, they can achieve.

MATH TEST

You are going to be taking a math test. I'd like you to prepare for that test now by taking time to relax and visualize a successful outcome. Lean back. Let your hands and arms go limp. Slowly close your eyes. Concentrate on your breathing. Pay attention to your stomach muscles as the air in your lungs forces them up and down. Breathe deeply and notice the differences in the size of your stomach. Feel the tension leave your body on the out breaths. (Allow one minute.)

Imagine now that you are taking the test. Watch on your giant TV screen as I pass out the papers. Notice how confidently you sit. You are alert, full of energy, and ready.

Watch as you turn your test paper over and begin working the problems. You breeze through the first one and go on to the next. The answers come easily for you. You are relaxed. Your attention is focused on the paper in front of you. You and the paper are one, working together to solve the problems. The problems are your friends and you enjoy them. You are having fun. Notice what it feels like to know you are doing well.

Enjoy that feeling. See yourself finishing the problems. Know that you have done well. You expect to get most of them correct. Enjoy the satisfaction. When you are ready, open your eyes and rejoin us. (Pause) Now let's take the test.

Test time can be anxiety-producing for students. This visualization is intended to soothe the mind and help erase worries and distractions. The relaxation activity alone is enough to improve test performance. Coupled with the positive picturing, you will get startling results.

How do you see yourself using this technique? Take a minute now to think it over. Use the following exercise to determine how you will fit it to you and your students.

List four occasions when you wished that students' behavior was more responsible, helpful, or cooperative. Your list might include

☆ When they switch from one activity to another
☆ When they come in from the lunchroom
☆ When a resource person comes to make a presentation
☆ When a substitute teacher comes in

List your four now.

Which one is most important to you? Which one, as you look them over, do you care most deeply about? Which one do you wish students had different pictures of in their minds? Write that one down.

Now take some time to design a positive picturing exercise for your students. Include relaxing, breathing deeply, picturing the desired process and result, feeling successful, and feeling strong positive emotions about being successful. Write the directions for your visualization now.

AFFIRMATIONS

In Chapter 8 we described how to use affirmations to arrange your own mind and to create your own reality. This same tool, the use of repetitious positive thought, can be used to help children move increasingly toward an "I Can" belief, "I Can" behaviors, and an "I Can" stance toward life.

Again, affirmation is a positive thought purposely placed in the mind to produce a desired result. Affirmations work because people eventually believe the messages they constantly send themselves. And they work whether or not a person is aware of the messages being sent.

So much of our lives, our experiences, and what we are is a result of the thoughts that we choose to hold in our minds. If a child's dominating thoughts are "I

169

can't," "I'm no good," "I'm fat and ugly," or "I'm a failure," his actions, behaviors, and life experiences will be markedly different from those of the child whose thoughts center around "I can," "I'm valuable," "I'm attractive," and "I'm successful."

Affirmations are a way to put each individual in control of those dominating thoughts. Affirmations are a way not to leave those thoughts to chance.

I can is an affirmation. If it, like other positive thoughts, is repeated often enough, it will sink into the subconscious mind and produce results consistent with the message sent. So will the following affirmations

☆ I am calm and relaxed during tests
☆ Learning is fun for me
☆ I work quickly with few errors
☆ My mind is powerful
☆ My memory is strong and helpful
☆ I find the correct answers at appropriate times
☆ I focus attention on one task at a time
☆ I am a good student
☆ Teachers like me
☆ I am friendly around my classmates

The above statements are examples of learning affirmations that will help students to believe in themselves, minimize self-doubt, and improve self-esteem. They are a powerful tool that can help you help your students learn, like themselves, and feel potent.

Affirmations are a way to help students move past limiting beliefs that have been suggested to them throughout their lives. Each of us has been conditioned to hold ideas that prevent us from reaching our potential. Affirmations can be that strategy to help students break limiting thought patterns, accelerate learning, and create the belief that more is possible.

Verbal Affirmations

Begin by choosing a couple of affirmations that you feel would be appropriate for students at your grade level. Word them in language your students recognize and understand. Explain to students that affirmations are a way of developing their minds by feeding in nutritious thoughts. The nutritious thoughts develop strong healthy minds like nutritious foods develop strong healthy bodies.

Two you may wish to begin with are

☆   I learn anything I decide to learn.

☆   I am an important member of our group.

Take about five minutes each morning to do affirmations. Have students relax. After you state the affirmation, have them repeat it out loud in unison. Do five or six repetitions with each one. Direct children to speak with emotion and strong feeling. Affirmations work faster and produce more noticeable results when emotion and strong feeling are attached to them.

Lee Ann Schlegel teaches hearing-impaired children in Michigan. To help her students overcome negative self-images and previous programming, Lee Ann facilitated the creation of a class creed. She explains,

> I told them a creed is something very good you know about yourself. I explained that nothing we wrote would be wrong because it was about us. Each child donated ideas and we built our creed.

> *The Class Creed*
> I am special.
> I am a good student.
> I can think.
> I can learn and understand.
> I can think for myself and nobody else.
> I can talk about many different things.
> I can have good speech and language.

> All these statements were positive things we felt about ourselves. I wrote our creed on poster board and put in on the wall. We read it every morning together and discuss briefly what it means. I sometimes ask after each line, "Are you special? Are you a good student?" They happily answer "Yes!" Sometimes I have them give an example.

> Now as we work they have replaced "I don't get it" with a positive statement that applies. I'm amazed at the results.

Written Affirmations

Students can also *write* affirmations. The positive statements can take the form of a penmanship lesson to be done while you meet with reading groups. A useful procedure is to have students write each affirmation once, repeat it silently to themselves, attach strong emotion to it, then repeat the process again with the same affirmation. Three or four repetitions are desirable before going on to the next one.

Each student you work with is unique. Each has skills, abilities, or personality traits he or she wants to improve. Some students want to get better at hitting baseballs, others at playing an instrument. Some students want to improve their spelling, others their memories. Other students want to have friends. Affirmations can be tailor-made to fit each individual.

Begin by asking students to think about what they want. Wants can include personality traits (positive, humorous, interesting), capabilities (good memory, fast runner, good reader), or outcomes (lots of friends, good report card, pleasing appearance). Ask them to list ten things they want. Have them narrow the list by picking their top five and then their top two. Their top two wants will be used for developing affirmations.

Using a top want, have students imagine themselves in a situation where the want already exists. If their want is to shoot baskets accurately, have them imagine themselves shooting baskets without a miss. If they want good memories, have them imagine themselves in situations where they use their memories successfully. Now have them each write a statement (affirmation) that describes how they have just imagined themselves.

☆ I shoot baskets accurately
☆ I have many friends
☆ My memory is useful

The next step in designing individual affirmations is for students to attach their names to the affirmations—immediately following the word *I* works well.

☆ I, Marge Bennet, shoot baskets accurately
☆ I, Roger Taynor, have an accurate memory

It is important that affirmations be positive and written as if the desired condition already exists. "I am able to shoot baskets accurately" is not as definite as "I shoot baskets accurately." "I'm getting a better memory" is not as final as "I have an accurate memory."

Total-class affirmations are useful in creating feelings of togetherness and potency. Done in unison, they have a magnetic effect that inspires confidence and faith.

☆ We are powerful.
☆ We, the Pink Panthers, are problem solvers.
☆ We are alive. We are alert. We are full of energy.

172

An appropriate time to express an affirmation orally is following a demonstration of the affirmation. If you have just finished a class meeting and solved a particularly sticky problem, that's a great time to chant "We are problem solvers. We never run out of ideas to solve problems." If students have successfully completed learning a new skill, that's an ideal occasion for affirming together, "We learn anything we decide to learn. We are powerful!"

"I Can" is more than a way of thinking, believing, and acting. It is a way of living. Through the use of "I Can" places, affirmations, positive picturing, and effective modeling, you will have an unending influence on the lives of your students. Begin now to strengthen your own "I Can-ness" and to develop ways to reach your students by using the following affirmation:

I, _____ , never run out of ways to teach children that they *can*!

SELF-AWARENESS: GLAD TO BE ME

The only person in the world I can change is myself. That is one of our basic beliefs. What follows from that belief is that the only person who can change a child is that child himself.

You may wish to change Robert's habit of putting himself down or Kirsten's odor or Rachel's seemingly uncontrollable chatter. The fact is that it's not possible. Only *they* can change. They make that choice no matter how hard and long you wish for them behavior, beliefs, or words that are more self-enhancing.

This is where self-awareness activities come in and why self-awareness activities are so critically important to Our Classroom teachers. Awareness is a link in the change process. Before a person moves actively to change something, that person must first be aware of what is, of what exists now. If Robert is not aware of the destructive nature of self-put-downs and the frequency with which he uses them, there is little chance he will change. If Kirsten is unaware of her odor and its effect on those near her, the likelihood of her altering the situation is slim.

With awareness comes a greater possibility for change. Kirsten may be all too aware of her odor and simply not care if she stinks. Robert may choose to keep right on whipping himself with derogatory remarks even after he learns about their frequency and their impact. Simple awareness is no guarantee that children will change, but it ups the odds.

We believe that self-growth and change begin with self-awareness and self-acceptance. If a person accepts himself where he is then he can use that as a base to grow away from. It is his support, his pillar to lean on while he takes some risks and begins to move slowly out of his comfort zone.

Without a base of self-acceptance, a person is not as likely to risk and grow. He is more likely to be busy defending himself or proving himself to himself and to others. Being in the midst of evaluating himself negatively or getting after himself is not a helpful place from which to change.

One category of self-awareness activities that Our Classroom teachers use with children are those designed to foster self-acceptance. These activities are created to help children examine themselves and enjoy what they see. These "Glad to Be Me" activities help children celebrate their uniqueness and their humanness.

Some "Glad to Be Me" activities follow.

CELEBRATE YOURSELF

Draw a large square with a small square inside of the larger one. Write in the small square your important strengths (positive factors). In the larger square, draw or paste pictures of these traits.

BUMPER STICKER

Design a bumper sticker to celebrate yourself. What would it look like? What would it say? Make one out of construction paper.

MILES OF SMILES

When do you smile? Draw a picture of your smile. Write in it a time you choose to smile. Post your smile on the "Miles of Smiles" board.

HIGH-FLYING KITES

Cut the body of a kite from construction paper. Divide it into four sections. In each section put a sentence, draw a picture, or cut out a picture from a magazine that represents

1.   Your family (upper left)
2.   Your home (upper right)
3.   Your special likes (lower left)
4.   Your wish for the future (lower right)

On each piece of the tail, list some ability you have that helps you fly high!

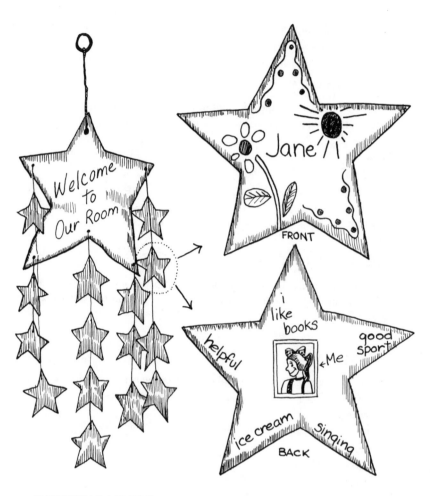

SUPERSTAR MOBILE

Sue Wolford, a Michigan teacher, has students create stars with their names on one side and their pictures on the other side. They then write five positive comments about themselves and put one on each point of the star. She attaches each star to a large star and hangs it near the doorway.

YOU ARE WHAT YOU EAT

Get a pile of old magazines. Have students cut and paste to create self-portraits using pictures of food they enjoy eating. Have them list the foods represented on their portraits by the four food groups. Have them determine which food group is represented the most and which the least.

THE NAME GAME

Write your name down the side of your paper. Think of positive words that describe you. Pick out words that start with the letters of your name.

S mart
H onest
E nergetic
I nspired
L aughing
A thletic

THE OTHER NAME GAME

Cut your name from a piece of construction paper and mount it on another piece of contrasting paper. Cover the name with drawings, cutouts, and actual things you like and enjoy.

SELF-COLLAGE

Self-collages can be created around a variety of themes. Some include

☆ My strengths
☆ Things I do well
☆ My feelings
☆ My goals
☆ My family

SELF-COMMERCIAL

Have students design commercials or advertisements about themselves stressing their most positive qualities.

GROWING

You know your body grows. You can see those results by comparing photos of yourself from year to year. Did you know that your mind grows right along with your body? You can tell it grows by the difference in your schoolwork. In kindergarten you probably couldn't read. Now you can. As your body has grown and changed, so has your mind.

Here are some ways to prove your mind has grown since you were in kindergarten.

1. List ten things you know now that you didn't know then.
2. Are you frightened of the same things now that you were then? Explain.
3. Write a story about a favorite toy that you've outgrown.
4. List three games you've outgrown. Write a paragraph about one of them.
5. How would you like your mind to grow in the next five years? Explain.

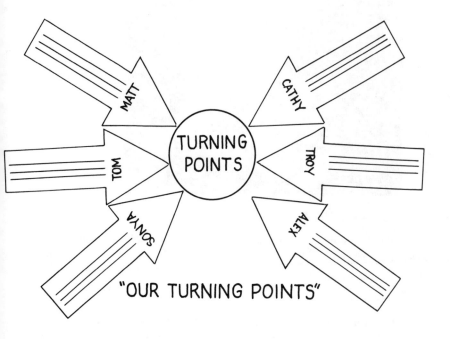

TURNING POINTS

Have students cut out large arrows from construction paper. Children identify one turning point in their lives they wish to share. They write that turning point on their arrow and add it to the turning point bulletin board.

USE YOUR HEAD

Sketch a profile of your head and cut it out. Block off two or three sections. What are your visions? What things do you plan to do in the future? Draw in your dreams.

SENSELESS

If you had to give up the use of one of your senses, which one would you choose? Would it be sight, touch, smell, taste, or hearing? Why did you choose the one you did? Which sense would you hate most to lose? Why?

TIME STUDY

How do you spend your time? Keep track of your time during a school day. Figure how many minutes you spend

178

☆ Working alone
☆ Working with others
☆ Playing alone
☆ Playing with others

Make a chart or a graph to display your data.

UP/DOWN

We all have ups and downs in our lives. What are two of yours? Fold a piece of construction paper in half. On one half draw a picture of a time when you were *up*. On the other half draw a picture of a time when you were *down*.

I STATEMENTS

Have children cut out large *I*'s from construction paper and divide them into several sections. Each section is then filled with an *I* statement and a picture.

SELF-AWARENESS EXTENSIONS

Self-awareness, "Glad to Be Me" activities, help students celebrate themselves and acquire a base of self-acceptance. Their value can be maximized, however, by an extension of the construction phase to include reflection, comparison, generalization, and goal setting. Certainly there is value in having students complete the suggested examples or others like them. There is also compounded value in designing ways for students to use those items once they have been constructed.

Display

The display of "Glad to Be Me" activities is one useful extension. Students see their place in the group; they have proof of their importance prominently featured; and the Our Classroom feeling is enhanced.

By displaying self-awareness activities the term *self*-awareness becomes a misnomer. In actuality, the phrase could be changed to *self- and other*-awareness. Not only do children learn about themselves, they learn about one another, too. Displaying these creations gives children the opportunity to view the work of their classmates as well as their own. Students get a clearer view of how they compare. Commonalities and uniquenesses can be discovered and appreciated.

Once self- and other-awareness activities are completed and on display, you can use them as the basis for class discussions, small-group discussions, journal writing, or other extensions. Here are some techniques for purposefully structuring follow-up activities to extend and expand the self-awareness lessons.

Class Discussions

Some students display their individual self-awareness contributions and show no interest in the work of their classmates. Generate interest by making it a minimum assignment to look over the work of others. Allow time for students to examine other creations. Have them write down their reactions and be ready to discuss them.

☆ Whose was most like yours?
☆ Whose was least like yours?

☆ Write down one thing you were surprised about on someone else's collage.

☆ What questions have been stimulated in your mind?

Ask open-ended questions when discussing self- and other-awareness activities. There are no wrong answers.

☆ Tell me what you noticed.

☆ Share one way our high-flying kites are alike.

☆ Tell something you learned looking at the helping hands.

At the conclusion of the discussion, collect student comments and post them near the display. This is a time to summarize and generalize.

Writing down students' comments ties the discussion together with a visible summary. It serves as a visual reminder of the things we talked about, learned, and re-learned.

Small-Group Discussions

Small-group discussions have an advantage over total-group discussions. More people get to talk more of the time. If you organize the class into six small discussion groups, then six people can talk at once as opposed to only one person talking in the large group.

Small-group discussions provide an opportunity for students to bring the "Glad to Be Me" activities to the group for closer self-examination and sharing. Design a structure that asks students to show and explain their creations. Students take turns responding to sentence starters.

☆ One thing I choose to share about my *I* statement is . . .

☆ Something about my Superstar-Mobile I'm proud of is . . .

☆ One thing that makes my snowflake different from everyone else's is . . .

After students respond orally, a give and take discussion follows. Students are encouraged to

☆ Ask questions of classmates

☆ Tell something they liked about someone else's contribution

☆ Share commonalities they noticed

☆ Give compliments and encouragement

Journals

Journals represent another delivery system for helping students extend interest in self-awareness activities. Students will often write something privately that they will not share orally. Journal time can be structured simply by stating

☆ Share with me something you learned or relearned about yourself today doing the self-commercial.

☆ Do you have any leftover thoughts about the kite activity we did this morning? If so, share them in your journal.

TOWARD CHANGE

The self-awareness activities presented so far help children examine their "good" qualities. They help students examine and celebrate the commonalities and differences inherent in humanness. These "Glad to Be Me" strategies help build a base of high self-esteem, positive regard, and self-acceptance.

It is also important that children become aware of the other side of themselves. There are personality traits, abilities, characteristics, and behaviors that they don't like. Some children believe they are lazy or uncreative, lack musical talent, or are uncoordinated. Some think they are fat, look unattractive, or have hot tempers.

Self-acceptance is important here, too. It continues to be true that the more children accept themselves as they are, the more likely they will be to change and grow from that spot.

Part of helping children deal with the other side of themselves is helping them with self-examination and personal goal setting. Many children haven't thought about abilities they would like to improve, personality traits they would like to strengthen, or characteristics they would like to develop. And if they don't know where they want to go, chances are they won't get there. Having children spend time wishing, dreaming, and thinking about their desires is a place to begin.

WISHING

Children have great imaginations. Put that ability to use by structuring times when it is legitimate for children to dream and wish. Often those wishes represent real desires that can lead to specific actions toward helpful growth.

Have students complete sentence starters like

☆ I wish I knew how to . . .

☆ I wish I had . . .

☆ I want to be able to . . .

☆ Something I want people to say about me is . . .

☆ I want people to like me for my . . .

GENIE IN THE BOTTLE

Bring in an old bottle. Tell students that there is a genie in it that often grants wishes. Open the bottle and ask children to write their top three wishes.

CREATIVE WRITING

Writing exercises often help children get in touch with their wants. Possible titles include

☆ I Wish I Were Someone Else

☆ Why You'd Like to Be Me

☆ A Wish Come True

☆ My Secret Ability

☆ I Wish I Could

WANT LISTS

Children can keep ongoing want lists in the back of their journals. The lists are divided into categories—things, abilities, and attitudes. The lists grow and evolve slowly over time.

GOAL SETTING

Helping children determine wants or desires is a first step toward change. No one changes unless he first has a desire to change. Once the desire is there, goal setting experiences help students clarify and attain those desires.

Resolutions

New Year's resolutions can be done anytime—today is always the beginning of a new year.

Have students write several resolutions concerning their behavior by listing new ways they wish to act. They then choose one to work with by underlining the resolution that's most important to them.

Explain that resolutions are actually goals. Because it is not possible to achieve a goal immediately, students *can* do activities that move them closer to that goal.

Help children appreciate the relationship between goals and do-able activities. Have them write their goals on paper and list activities that will help them achieve the goals. Students working in trios can help one another by offering suggested activities to add to the lists.

For instance, a child's goal may be to get 100 percent correct on a spelling test. Activities that will help the student move closer to the desired goal could include

☆ Writing each word ten times
☆ Having a friend give a trial test
☆ Spelling each word out loud three times
☆ Taking tricky words home to study

Although it may not be possible to achieve the *goal* immediately, it is possible to do the *activities* that will result in eventual realization of the goal.

Journals

Keeping goals in journals is one way students can monitor their own efforts. Friday's journal entry could be a reflection on the week.

☆ What did you do this week to move you closer to your goal?
☆ What will you do next week?
☆ How do you like your goal now?

A special Growth Book can be used for this specific purpose. Students use it to record dreams, wishes, wants, goals, activities, accomplishments, feelings. Imagine the empowering feelings generated by looking back over several months' worth of growth and accomplishment!

GOAL POSTS

Jack Canfield and Paula Klimek suggest decorating a bulletin board in the form of a goalpost.[2] Students begin their day by each writing a goal. The individual goals are placed on file cards and added to the bulletin board below the crossbar.

[2]Jack Canfield and Paula Klimek, "Teaching Human Beings to Love Themselves," in *Self Concept Sourcebook*, ed. Dov Peretz Elkins (Rochester, NY: Growth Associates, 1979), pp. 191–210.

Students move their cards above the goal post whenever they accomplish their goals. This immediate visible reinforcement is highly motivational and satisfaction producing.

I'D LIKE TO/I CAN

Divide a bulletin board in half. Label one side "I'd Like to" and the other side "I Can." Have students set goals for themselves of something they'd like to do. Have them write their goals on file cards and place them upside down on the side labeled "I'd Like to." Students write their names on the side of the cards that is showing. When students achieve their "I'd Like tos," they remove the cards from that side of the board, turn them over, and place them on the "I Can" side. Students set as many goals as they choose.

ATMOSPHERE
OF ACCEPTANCE

Encouraging children to engage in self-improvement begins with an inviting atmosphere. Children will accept more invitations to "try on" new behaviors, new acts, and new ways of looking at things if the classroom climate is positive, warm, and supportive. Self-examination, growth, and change occur more often in an atmosphere of acceptance where children can make mistakes, get feedback on those mistakes, and risk change without feeling defeated. Teachers are primarily responsible for creating that environment.

Mind Arrangement

Because acceptance is a mind skill, begin to create an environment of acceptance by arranging your own mind. Once your mind is tuned into acceptance, appropriate strategies, techniques, ideas, and language will flow.

It is easy to become impatient with a child who often interrupts or picks his nose until it bleeds. It is easy to be exasperated with a student who gives up easily, doesn't follow through, or lies a lot. And it's easy to get discouraged with a child who fights once a week or pouts when things don't go her way.

It can be difficult to accept fighting, pouting, lying, and other behaviors you prefer didn't exist. And we're not suggesting that you do! We're not saying that you have to accept or even tolerate those behaviors. We are saying it is critical that you accept the child who on occasion chooses those behaviors.

☆ You can accept a child who lies without liking, accepting, or tolerating the lying

☆ You can accept a child who whines without liking, accepting, or tolerating the whining

☆ You can accept a child who fights without liking, accepting, or tolerating the fighting

The key to accepting a person who exhibits unacceptable behavior lies in your mind. There are two mind skills you can use to accept children regardless of their behavior.

The first skill involves separating the child from the behavior. The child is *not* the behavior. As long as you see the child as the behavior, you will have trouble accepting the child. The more you see the undesired behavior as only one aspect of a fully functioning human being capable of thousands of different behaviors and feelings, the more accepting you will feel toward the person.

GUIDED IMAGERY

Think of a child whose behavior has given you trouble liking her as a person. Got one in mind? (Read through this exercise before you begin.)

Relax and close your eyes. Concentrate on your breathing. Count your breaths as you breathe deeper and deeper. When you are breathing deeply and rhythmically, picture the child. See her doing the behavior you dislike. Monitor your feelings while you watch with your mind's eye as the child continues the behavior. Zoom in close with your high-powered lens. See the child as the behavior. Equate the child with the behavior. Label her as the behavior. Write a label and stick it on her. Now back up and watch the child from farther away. Notice the label. The child *is* the behavior. Write your feelings now about this child.

Once again relax and breathe deeply. Do as you did a minute ago to ensure deep rhythmic breathing. When you are ready, picture the child again with your mind's eye. See her doing the behavior. Now begin to back up with your inner camera. Begin to stretch the child. See her as a wide range of behaviors and attitudes. Notice many things about her. See her as someone who employs many behaviors in many situations. See this person as someone's child and someone's sister. See her fears, humor, misconceptions. Notice her as serious and as playful. Notice her giving, regret, worry. Widen this person and experience her as a wide spectrum of thoughts, behaviors, and attitudes. Now record your feelings about the child.

If you hang on to the narrow view of this person and see her as the behavior, you will have trouble accepting her. On the other hand, if you arrange your mind to perceive her as larger than the behavior, you will have an easier time with acceptance. Use this mind skill to help you accept those children you've had trouble seeing positively. Our hunch is that you will surprise yourself with the results you get.

PIP

Another useful way to perceive children with behaviors you don't enjoy is to see them as Persons in Progress (PIP). We are all imperfect and unfinished. We are all, as Carl Rogers says, Persons in Progress. You can choose to see being unfinished as a catastrophe or you can choose to see it as an opportunity, as a chance to help a child learn and grow. How you see imperfection is up to you.

If you learn to see children as Persons in Progress, you will be more accepting of them as people. You will teach them by your example and attitude that they are OK even though they are unfinished. You will create an environment of acceptance in which children are more likely to perceive their own imperfections as opportunities for change and growth.

Activities that Foster Acceptance

An environment of acceptance can also be enhanced by structuring in specific activities, lessons, and areas within the classroom that help produce the desired climate. By your choice of materials and strategies, you affect the emotional temperature of your classroom. It is your responsibility to regulate that temperature. To move your climate in the direction of increased warmth and positiveness, consider the following.

UNBIRTHDAY

Some children have birthdays during the summer. Are they forgotten in the September-to-June school year? How about holding unbirthday parties for these students? Let them choose the date.

COMPLIMENT BOX

Decorate a small box. Invite students to drop in compliments for others in the classroom. Locate the Compliment Box close to the line-up area, and make it a practice to read the compliments aloud to the waiting group.

FAMILY OF THE WEEK

Each student (as well as the teacher) is assigned one week during the school year when she becomes the focus of Family of the Week. During that week, the student assumes additional responsibilities, such as line leader, special helper, errand runner. Also during that week an entire bulletin board is set aside for that child and her family. A display is created from items selected by the child including

☆ Family photos
☆ Evidence of special talents
☆ Family pets
☆ Mementos from trips or special occasions
☆ Favorite foods
☆ Collections

Parents are asked to help children select items, which are sent to school on Monday of that special week. They stay on display until Friday.

In addition, the entire family is invited in during the week to meet with the class. Parents share stories about the child, interesting family traditions, and information about occupations.

BABY PHOTOS

Have children bring in baby pictures. When several have been brought to school, start a mystery person board. One Monday put up an unidentified photo. Encourage children to look it over and guess who it is. Each succeeding day add a clue. Clues can include interests, hobbies, characteristics, and so on.

Monday	Post the photo
Tuesday	"Loves to play softball"
Wednesday	"Has brown eyes"
Thursday	"Belongs to Girl Scout Troop 98"
Friday	"Walks to school"

LOOK WHO'S SPECIAL

Judy Brandt, a Kalamazoo, Michigan, teacher, created a "Look Who's Special" bulletin board. It was her way of encouraging positiveness and discouraging tattling among her kindergarten students.

Judy kicked off this special project with a class discussion on what a special person might be or do. The five- and six-year-olds responded with ideas including (1) someone who shares with me; (2) someone who does nice things for me; (3) someone who helps me with something; (4) someone who's doing better or improving.

Discussing special people helped children grow in recognizing special contributions from classmates. The discussion was so helpful that Judy decided to add permanence to the activity. She created a special bulletin board and structured a daily sharing of positive comments.

Judy organized it so that children came together at the end of their day for a class meeting. At this time they shared nice things that happened to them that day and observations of nice things that happened to others. They shared comments like

☆ Tonya helped Heidi take off her boots.
☆ Anthony knew his letter pictures today.
☆ Heidi shared her scissors.
☆ Becky helped Walter unbuckle his boots.

As students shared, Judy wrote. She recorded the comments word for word. The comments were added to the board under the name of the child who was observed being special. Each person had his own spot on the bulletin board marked with a self-portrait and special gold paper.

Two limitations governed the possible responses. No one could comment about himself; all contributions had to be observations of others. And remarks had to come from children, not from the teacher.

Not every student commented every day, and not every student had a comment made about her every day. But Judy was careful to see that everyone did participate and that everyone was included at some time.

At any time during the school day children could glance at the board and see written proof of their positive presence in that classroom. They could see the list of items others had suggested about them.

When a child's gold paper was filled with comments, it came down and a new blank sheet went up. The list of positive observations was folded in half and fastened carefully with a gold seal. The "special" message was then sent home to be shared.

As a result of the project, positive communication increased within the kindergarten classroom. Children said more nice things about one another. Judy had found a special way to help kids feel special.

WELCOMES AND SEND-OFFS

What do you do for students who move during the year and go to another school? How do you welcome a new student? Why not put these issues to the children? Ask for their ideas. Let them design a strategy for seeing that welcomes and send-offs are not left to chance.

Anti-Put-Down Strategies

Student are masters at the technique of put-downs. Put-downs, derogatory remarks about yourself or others, can take the form of out loud taunts ("You dummy") or inside thoughts ("I'm no good"). Regardless of the form they take, put-downs are divisive and unhealthy; they work against self-acceptance and an Our Classroom environment.

Our Classroom teachers, therefore, employ anti-put-down strategies to alleviate this destructive behavior. Some of the strategies follow.

FUNERAL

Hold a put-down funeral. Have students write as many self-put-downs as they can think of. All put-downs are placed in a shoebox, taken to the playground, and buried. They are never used again. They are dead.

NO MATTER

Teach children the following mind skill.[3] Whenever anyone shouts an insult at them or puts them down, they repeat immediately to themselves, "No matter what you say or do, I'm still a worthwhile person." Practice this with your students by having insult sessions. Shout insults at them like

☆ This is the dumbest class I have ever had.
☆ You're all out of shape.
☆ All you eat is junk food.
☆ You must have a pea for a brain.

At the end of each insult they respond in unison with "No matter what you say or do, I'm still a worthwhile person."

It is important that children learn to use this skill inside their heads, in the privacy of their own minds. One teacher reported teaching this to her class as a coping mechanism. A child repeated the phrase out loud to his mother after he had been called lazy and received a slap in the face. Teach your children to use this tool in their minds.

[3]Elkins, *Teaching People to Love Themselves*, p. 94.

IALAC

This is the story of a student who wore an IALAC sign around all day.[4] (IALAC stands for "I Am Lovable and Capable.") As he progressed throughout the day, his lovableness and capableness were ripped away piece by piece. *I Am Loveable and Capable* by Sid Simon is a useful way to share the notion of put-downs with young children.

AFFIRMATIONS

Teach children to use affirmations to cancel out put-downs. Whenever students catch a self-put-down, they follow it with an affirmation. The affirmation is an effective antidote and cancels the put-down.

☆ "I'm no good" is followed by "I have lots of strengths."

☆ "I'm lazy" is followed by "I work hard on things I care about."

☆ "What a klutz" is followed by "My body is a marvelous machine, capable of thousands of beautiful movements."

WARM-FUZZY AREAS

A warm-fuzzy is a compliment (written or oral) given to another person. A warm-fuzzy area is one purposefully created to increase the exchange of warm-fuzzies.

[4]Sidney B. Simon, *I Am Loveable and Capable* (Allen, TX: Argus Communications, 1973).

Begin a warm-fuzzy clothesline in your classroom. Have students decorate clothespins in their own images and write their names on them. Hang them on the line next to yours. Students use these mini-mailboxes to share positive notes with one another. Model this technique by sending at least three warm-fuzzies a day yourself.

How about a warm-fuzzy clothesline for your staff room? Teachers, administrators, secretaries, cooks, custodians, and other members of the school family enjoy compliments, encouragement, and special interest. Why not create a delivery system for that warmth and caring? Help create the Our Staff feeling.

GROWING FRIENDSHIP TREE

Michigan teacher Sue Wolford developed the Growing Friendship Tree. Her directions follow.

Make a tree and an apple for each student. The apple is actually a pocket for nice notes. Each day everyone is asked to write a *positive* comment or make a nice picture for someone else in the class. These notes do not have to be signed. We hope this activity will become a habit, done every day for a different friend. Friendships develop and ripen like fruit, but it takes time.

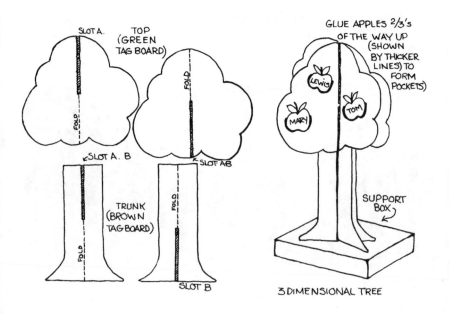

This chapter has been about strengthening notions of "our" by strengthening individuals. In it we stressed the importance of children seeing themselves as able, valuable, and responsible. We shared a variety of ideas and strategies that help produce healthy, positive environments for children. What we haven't shared yet and have saved for the finale may well be one of the most critical aspects of creating an Our Classroom feeling—*you*.

You, the teacher, are the key. You, your way of looking at things, your way of operating, your example as a living, functioning human being have a major impact on the children you work with, the type of environment you create, and the degree of Our Classroom feeling that results.

In Chapter 11 we focus on *you* and *your* role in creating the Our Classroom feeling.

11

the teacher is the message

No printed word nor spoken plea can teach young minds what men could be,
Not all the books on all the shelves but what the teachers are themselves.

ANONYMOUS

As I think about the children I taught, I don't believe they took a year of fifth grade from
me. I believe they took a year of me for fifth grade.

Those are the words of Dr. Hanoch McCarty of Cleveland State University. He
shared that thought with us and other participants during one of the many workshops
he conducts on affective education.

When I heard him share that message, I immediately thought back to my fifth-
grade teaching experiences and realized that he was correct. The students I had as
fifth graders didn't get fifth grade from me either. They got me. Likewise, your students aren't taking second grade or fourth grade or kindergarten. They are taking
you.

Think about it. Your classroom is you. Your language is you. The materials
you select to use with students are you. Everything that goes on in that classroom is
strongly flavored with huge doses of you. You don't give students a year of second
grade. You give them a year of you.

You, the teacher, and you, the human being, have an enormous impact on the
students you teach. Are you conscious of the silent messages your behavior sends to
children? Are you aware of what you model? Do you choose your modeling with intentionality? Is that important to you?

Are you aware of the degree to which you share your humanness with students? Do you do it on purpose? Have you developed ways to be real with students that help them connect to your humanness? Do you drop the facade of professional teacher and let students see pieces of you, the human being? Do you want to?

The main premise of this chapter is that you, the teacher, are your own best resource. True, it is primarily the board of education that makes curriculum, spending, and hiring decisions. The principal generally decides class lists, assigns rooms, and sets procedures. Committees often make textbook recommendations, decide report card formats, and create curriculum guides for each grade level. Yet you alone close that door behind you and face a classroom full of children. You share a year full of experiences with your students.

You offer students textbooks, manipulatives, and learning tasks of every size, shape, and content. You offer them choices, rewards, and opportunities to solve problems. You offer them consequences, chances to accept responsibility, and opportunities for input. Yet the most important thing you have to offer your students is your own humanity. When you give of yourself you give something that is real, something that no one else can offer. You offer you.

How do you set it up so that students can share in that most valuable resource? Do you have an organized plan to do that? Do you have any strategies, ideas, and delivery systems already in use? Following are some ideas we have seen others use. Think about them. See if they have meaning for you.

SHARING YOURSELF

Barb Hines, a third-grade teacher, made a scrapbook of herself, brought it to school, and shared it with her students. She did it because she wanted to appear more human to her students. According to Barb,

> So many times our students forget we are human, and many times I think we as teachers forget we are human also. I wanted my students to see that I'm just like they are and that I have feelings probably much like theirs.
>
> To help our class see more of my humanness I made a book called *Meet the Real Barb Hines*. The book is divided into two sections. Section I is a brief autobiography and contains background information on my birth, family, schooling, job, home, husband, and children. This section is filled with baby pictures and other pictures pertaining to my life.
>
> Section II deals with me as I am now, including information on height, weight, coloring, et cetera. Also included in this part of the book is a sharing of times when I feel sad, happy, and angry; when I want to be with friends; things I've learned; when I want to be alone; my favorite things; and many other topics.

A variation of this self-sharing strategy was done by a kindergarten teacher who attended one of our workshops. She, too, created a scrapbook about herself, but included only one picture per page. Her directions to the youngsters were "Pick a picture and I'll tell you a story about myself." One picture showed her family, another a pet. Some revealed places she had traveled. Others showed significant happenings in her childhood. Once a week children would choose a picture, then listen intently as this teacher shared a personal story explaining the picture.

Mary Chapoton, a first-grade teacher, took children to her apartment for lunch. She took them in groups of six over a three-week period. The menu included hot dogs, chips, cookies, and Kool-Aid. Mary, who lives within easy driving distance of school, explained, "They had no conception of how I lived. Plus I like to see as many sides of them as possible. And I like them to do the same with me."

One upper-elementary teacher shared some of his humanness with students through a photo cube. The cube was filled with photos showing scenes from his personal life. He changed the photos frequently and answered questions from interested students.

How about a bulletin board that features you? You could be the first "Person of the Week." Include some photos, drawings, magazine clippings, and souvenirs of highlights of your life. Share about your family, childhood, hobbies, trips, hopes, likes, dislikes, and talents. Your sharing serves as a model for each "Person of the Week" who follows.

My last two years in the classroom I used a strategy I termed "Ask Me." It was time set aside for children to interview me, press-conference style. They could ask me anything they wanted. If I chose not to answer a question, I told them why.

Students' questions were basic at first

- ☆ Do you have any brothers and sisters?
- ☆ How old are you?
- ☆ Are you a Republican or a Democrat?

As the trust level grew between us, so did the depth of the questions.

- ☆ Do you like giving grades?
- ☆ When did you decide to be a teacher?
- ☆ Do you tell other people about us sometimes?
- ☆ Do you like being you?

This exercise helped us to be genuine with one another. It helped dissolve the walls between teacher and students and fostered mutual respect. I found that children consistently took this activity seriously and looked forward to it. So did I.

Another strategy for letting children glimpse your humanity is to bring things that interest you into the classroom. What are your interests—baseball cards, political buttons, macrame, orchids, books? Your special interest offers a personal link between you and the child. It matters less *what* you share. It matters more *that* you share it.

One sixth-grade teacher we talked to shares herself by bringing her guitar into the classroom. As she told us,

> My guitar is a part of me not easily shared with others. It is a dimension of me that few people know. I play and sing with adults, but I'm not sharing that special feeling. I come closer to it when I play for kids. They accept what is offered with no expectations. I share what I am.
>
> In school I sit and play whenever and wherever I get the urge. The kids sense whether I am in the mood for a sing-along or whether I am privately exploring and enjoying my music. They know that either way they are free to share the experience or go on about their business.
>
> After I sing a song for them and they follow along with the words, we discuss our favorite phrases. It was an incredible experience to have a child tell me what part she thought I liked best even before I realized it myself. I was delighted! At least one person had learned something about me with no words necessary.

Obviously not everyone has a guitar to share, but we all have something. Every one of us has found meaning in our life and can share that with our students. Share those experiences that matter to you. Invite your class to catch a glimpse of what is important in your life.

One teacher who cared deeply about animals held an Endangered Species Day. Another shared summer travel experiences through slide presentations. Still another teacher shared her interest in insects by bringing her collection to school.

A fifth-grade teacher who is a runner used his lunch periods to jog around the school property. He invited interested students to join him. Not everyone accepted the invitation. Those who did jogged along sharing health and conversation with their teacher. Those who didn't could still see visible proof of an adult putting his beliefs and interests into action day after day.

Photography is something I enjoy. When my interest in photography was first budding, I shared it with students. Because I was enthusiastic about it, they picked up on that enthusiasm, and many of them got excited about it too. We made slide-tape shows and photograph collages and created collections of our memories.

I don't know if any of those students ever went any deeper into photography as a hobby or as a vocation. And it doesn't matter. What does matter is that they saw a teacher who enjoyed something so much that he wanted to share it with others. They saw a teacher who was in the process of learning and turning out rejects as regularly as keepers. They saw a teacher who was enthusiastic and full of energy over something new in his life. They saw a piece of me.

Sharing Yourself Planning Guide

There is something meaningful in your life waiting to be shared with your students. And only *you* know what it is! Take the time to find it now.

List five things you care deeply about. These can be political issues, people, projects, attitudes. Do it now.

List five topics you know something about. You don't have to be an expert on these issues, you just have to know something about them. These can be hobbies, places, interests, or whatever. Do it now.

List five things you have learned in your life that you believe are worth sharing. What would you like people to know about the way you have come to understand the world? List those learnings now.

Now go back over your lists. Cross off any items you would not feel comfortable sharing with students. Cross off any that would be expensive to share. Eliminate any items that would require more time than you are willing to spend.

Now look over the remaining items. Read each out loud. As you focus on the page, one or two items will stand out. One, two, and sometimes even three will signal to you that they want to be picked. Trust your gut level feelings. Circle the one, two, or three that are signaling to you.

The items you have circled are an ideal place to begin connecting with students. They are items you care deeply about, know something about, or believe are worth sharing. If your feelings are that strong concerning these items, you owe it to your students and to yourself to share with them.

How will you share these items with students? Design a plan for yourself now. List each one on a single sheet of paper. Work with one at a time. List all thoughts and ideas that come to your mind about sharing. Include ways to share, items to share, fears, and concerns about sharing. When you have filled your paper, turn it over and write a two-sentence statement that describes what you will do.

Do this for all three items. Pick one and implement. Make a date to check with yourself one week later to see how you did.

"BEING WITH" STUDENTS

One of the best ways to share *you* with youngsters is to arrange activities and processes so that you can *be with* your students. Many times teachers are so busy "do-

ing to" students that they don't have time to "be with" them. "Doing to" students is a way of maintaining distance. "Being with" students is a way of narrowing that distance.

"Being with" students means arranging some time when you aren't busy administering, evaluating, observing, recording, praising, suggesting, solving, or managing. "Being with" means hanging out and being around children. It means being there to interact, to joke and laugh, to play, to work, to share, to connect.

The playground is a reasonable place to "be with" children. They're different out there than they are in the classroom. You know that, but how often do you observe it up close? How often do you program that experience into your schedule?

Hang out on the playground once in a while. Not every day. Your breaks are valuable too. Don't do it on days when you're on duty. Do it on other days when you're free to roam around.

Journeying onto the playground is a way of reaching out that meets children on their territory. Once a week or so skip rope, join a softball game, play catch. Trade baseball cards, roll marbles, or hold coats. Be there!

Lunchtime is another interesting time to be with students. Try out the lunchroom or invite students to eat with you. As a teacher I enjoyed a quiet lunch away from a crowded lunchroom. On occasion I invited a handful of students to join me in the classroom for lunch. We sat and talked quietly. I found the less I talked the more I learned, and the more I talked the less I learned. We suggest you do this once a week early in the year until everyone gets a turn. Our hunch is that you will enjoy it so much that you'll do it again later in the year.

Our Classroom teachers often go out of their way to arrange special times to be with students outside as well as inside school. Donna Mygrants is one teacher who did just that. She took her fifth graders to a local roller skating rink, found a nice spot to sit near the concession stand, and watched. She described what followed this way.

I sat down with a glass of root beer and began to observe my students outside the classroom. Every one of those kids was out there skating. At the time I was surprised to see so much enthusiasm and laughing and falling down, getting up, and trying again. What amazed me was that this scene was different from the normal everyday classroom epic. Not one of my students sat on the sidelines and watched. Not one of these kids was unable to get out there. All of them—even my most uncoordinated student—were out on the rink trying and having fun. I realized I was the only one from our class not out there. So then and there I made the transition. I put my root beer down, took a deep breath, skated onto the rink, got rid of my teacher role and became a learner. My kids taught me how to skate!

It's difficult to put into words the expressions on some of the faces of my students when they saw that I couldn't do something. Some joked and kidded, others were concerned, still others skeptical.

Throughout the year that special day was continually brought up. "Remember when Mrs. Mygrants flew into Mr. Wippel (our principal) when she was at the end of the whip and when she almost banged right into the wall? Good thing we were there to show you how, huh, Mrs. Mygrants?"

Although we joked and laughed about my experiences, I realized how important it was for my kids to see something I didn't know that they knew.

☆ We have seen teachers drive students downtown to buy tropical fish for the aquarium or purchase snacks for the Valentine's party.

☆ We have noticed teachers organize and supervise model rocket clubs as well as woodworking and sand-sculpture activities after school.

☆ We have watched teachers monitor chess and checker tournaments on their lunch hours.

☆ We have seen hours of effort by teachers staging plays, skits, pageants, and choral presentations with their students.

☆ We have witnessed teachers giving time, effort, and energy to arrange for students to visit a bank, a fire station, or a bakery.

☆ We have observed teachers painting scenery, working on relief maps, and assisting with party decorations.

☆ We have seen teachers make home visits to their students before the school year begins.

Every time I see or hear teachers sharing and caring that little bit extra, I'm reminded of what Vickie Dove-Winfield told me when I asked her why she went to the trouble to organize, finance, and supervise an all-day trip to Chicago for her students. She looked me right in the eye and said, "I didn't do it *for* them. I did it *with* them."

Another way to be with children is to do activities with them. If students are constructing a self-collage, you make a self-collage. If the class is working on a giant puzzle, add a few pieces to it yourself. Add your link to the goal chain, your page to the favorite sandwich book, your opinion to the opinion collection. Join in.

In Our Classroom, *all* members are asked to share thoughts, feelings, attitudes, beliefs, likes, and dislikes. Every day we ask students to discuss, draw, sculpt, color, or write about themselves. If we're in the business of asking children to share parts of themselves with us, then it's important for us to model that message.

Be the "Person of the Week," add to the Proud Board, display one of your success objects. Show students your willingness to risk sharing opinions, beliefs, fears, and hopes. When your self-portrait is part of a wall divider, when your baby picture is part of a display entitled "Remember When," when the piece of green moss attached to the "Our Color Walk" bulletin board has been placed there by you, then the message is clear—everyone is willing to risk and share in Our Classroom.

Planning to
"Be with" Students

What ways do you have to "be with" students? Does it occur by accident, or do you purposefully structure to see that it happens? Do you do it with regularity, or is it a spontaneous occurrence?

What do *you* want in this area of "being with"/"doing to" students? Write a one-sentence "want" statement now.

Because you are the one responsible for getting your wants met, how are you going to do that? What are three things you will do *this week* to move you closer to realizing your want? List them on your paper.

ACTING AS A MODEL

In his workshops with teachers, Ed Frierson tells the story of the veteran teacher who hated gum. As gum haters go, this woman was in the ninety-ninth percentile. Her students loved to chew gum. And because the sight, smell, or sound of gum was a constant irritant to this teacher, she tried to prevent her students from engaging in what she interpreted as a nasty habit.

This anti-gum-chewing teacher lectured her students, using statistics about germs, tooth decay, and the cost of dental work. The students chewed on. She moralized about manners, respect, and simple decency. Still they chewed. She scolded and reprimanded in different tones of voice. The children never wavered. She used threat, punishment, and removal of privileges. The gum chewing continued.

This woman tried every way she knew to convince students to stop chewing gum. Her explanations, opinions, and desires continued to be ignored. So she gave up trying to get through to her students with logic and persuasion.

One day a child arrived at school early and found her chipping gum from beneath desks with a putty knife. "What are you doing?" the student asked. "Getting rid of the gum," she replied. "I hate gum and don't like it on the furniture."

After watching the teacher chip gum from the bottom of desks for three mornings in a row, the student asked if he could help. The teacher produced a second putty knife and together they passed the time until school started by steadily removing gum from desks.

The next day a second child asked to help. The work force grew until ten children were removing gum from furniture. A few days later the room was void of gummed desks and the crew moved to the school library. When the library was cleared of gummed furniture, they moved on to the lunchroom. Within three weeks all the furniture in the entire school had become gum-free.

Children in this classroom stopped chewing gum, and they did it on their own without being threatened, lectured to, or punished. They stopped because they could see gum chewing meant something to their teacher. They could tell that she felt strongly about her conviction because she chose to act and thus lived out her values and beliefs. They could see by her demonstration how important the issue of gum chewing was to her.

This story can be summed up by an anonymous quotation we heard some time ago: "Attitudes are more easily caught than taught." When the teacher tried to teach non-gum-chewing, she was unsuccessful. The children turned her off. When she switched to action and modeled her beliefs, they tuned in and responded accordingly.

We believe children have built in "on" and "off" knobs over which they have complete control. It seems easy for them to turn us off and let our words roll off their backs. Lecturing, moralizing, judging, and criticizing don't get through when children choose not to let it in. Far better to take a lesson from the gum hater and let our actions be our message.

Our Classroom teachers know they are models. They realize they are being watched. And they are absolutely aware that their styles of teaching and living have impact on those around them. And because Our Classroom teachers know their attitudes are being caught, they consciously model.

Our Classroom teachers model appreciation. Nancy Clark, a kindergarten teacher we work with, keeps a "Thank You" Chart. Students' names and reasons for appreciation are shared on the chart whenever it's appropriate. The chart becomes a permanent, visible record of gratitude and appreciation. Nancy believes that children learn to appreciate by being appreciated.

The following note was found in another Our Classroom environment.

Dear Tim:

Thanks a whole lot for bringing in your workbench to share with the room. It will get a whole lot of use during the year I'm sure. We can probably begin to use it in a week or two.

Mr. R

The principal of an elementary school posted the following invitation on an empty bulletin board in the lobby:

Write a note to our custodians. Tell them something you like about our building.

Several children accepted the invitation.

Thank you for fixing the part that had the crack on the merry-go-round.

Joey

Thanks for cleaning our rug. I like it that you are making the valley slides.

Brooke

Thank you for fixing the tire sculpture.

Laura

Our Classroom teachers model sharing their feelings. When they are angry they say so. When they like someone, they express their liking. When they feel frustrated, they verbalize it. When they are excited they share it.

And Our Classroom teachers own their feelings. They don't say, "You make me happy." They say, "I'm feeling happy," and take full responsibility for those feelings.

They say, "I'm choosing to be angry," instead of "You make me angry."

They say, "I'm upset," instead of "You're upsetting me."

They say, "I appreciate your help," instead of "You are a good girl."

In short, they use language that tells how they are feeling, experiencing, or perceiving. Their language tells about *them*.

Our Classroom teachers also model imperfection. When they make mistakes in front of children they accept their mistakes as evidence of their humanness. They believe that error by the teacher has value. They know they aren't perfect and don't pretend they are. They are at peace with their imperfections and aren't afraid to reveal them.

In an Our Classroom environment the teacher is a learner too. Our Classroom teachers are busy learning about children, their profession, and themselves. If they take graduate classes they talk about their experiences, sharing joys and frustrations. If they are practicing a new skill, such as guitar or macrame, they share their struggle and their accomplishments. Our Classroom teachers model learning as a lifelong process.

By modeling the qualities they believe in, Our Classroom teachers purposefully influence their students. They know that concepts like conviction, initiative, caring, honesty, and respect aren't taught. They know these qualities begin to develop in children when they encounter others who possess them. To notice honesty, caring, or respect in another person is inspirational. Observing a trait in another person is a step on the path to development of that trait.

What Do You Model?

Think about your time with children. What are children learning about cooperation or competition by watching you? What conclusions are they drawing about criticism or acceptance by watching you? What do you teach about "I Can-ness" by how you live your life? What do you visibly do that inspires sharing, service, or support? What do you model?

Your students are watching you. What are they learning about how you react to problems and frustrations? Does the immaturity of your students bring out the immaturity of their teacher? Or do you model being centered and not taking things personally? Are your students witnessing an ongoing clinic in the beauty of problem solving, or are they learning to blame and punish?

What do you communicate to students by how you live your school life? Do you just talk about the importance of goal setting, or are goals an integral and visible part of your day? Do you only show movies about the necessity of people getting along, or do you cultivate warm, visible relationships with other staff members? Do you model going the extra mile, or is your approach to complain when others don't?

Your children are watching—seeing what is important and real to you. Are they seeing what you want them to see? What do you model? What do others learn from the way you live your life? What do the people who watch you say about you? Take some time to consider these questions by completing the following sentence starters:

☆ Children see that I . . .
☆ Other teachers notice my . . .
☆ I show that I care about . . . by . . .
☆ Teachers know that . . . is important to me because . . .
☆ The three values I model most consistently are . . .
☆ One thing I would like to do differently in front of my students is . . .
☆ One belief I want to make more visible is . . .
☆ I will do that by . . .

CONCLUSION

There is no right way to teach. There is no one right way to be an Our Classroom practitioner. The role will always remain as unique as the teacher who fills it. And that's as it should be.

The ideas presented in this book are only some of the many available that can help you create an Our Classroom feeling. They do not constitute the final answer or even the best answer for everyone. The ideas we have shared are a jumping-off place, a place to begin. They are only part of *your* answer.

Our Classroom teachers believe in different right answers for children and they believe in different right answers for themselves. They trust their own judgment to choose from the variety of technology, theory, and strategies that are available and to find what is right for them as individual teachers.

Our Classroom teachers trust their intuition. They believe they know at a gut level what works best with children and aren't afraid to follow hunches. Several teachers we work with, when asked to explain why they used a particular strategy, were not able to articulate a rational, logical reason. "It seemed right," they say, or "It feels good." More often than not, teachers who reported going with their hunches also reported that that activity or decision turned out to be the most exciting and helpful strategy they implemented all week. Our Classroom teachers believe in themselves enough to do what they think and feel is best. They trust that they know.

We hope that you will take these ideas, thoughts, and strategies and fit them to you. Change them around until they feel appropriate for your grade level, your children, and you. Use them, change them, and add to them to help you be all that you want to be as a teacher and as a person. Enjoy!

bibliography

Although the majority of material in this book comes from personal contact with educators, direct observation of classrooms, and our own experience, we found the following books helpful. We suggest them to you for your consideration as tools to help you support and extend what you already do as an Our Classroom practitioner.

CANFIELD, JACK, and HAROLD WELLS. *100 Ways to Enhance Self-Concept in the Classroom.* Englewood Cliffs, NJ: Prentice-Hall, Inc., 1976.

CASTEEL, J. DOYLE. *Learning to Think and Choose.* Pacific Palisades, CA: Goodyear Publishing Co., 1978.

CHENFELD, MIMI BRODSKY. *Teaching Language Arts Creatively.* New York, NY: Harcourt Brace Jovanovich, Inc., 1978.

CLEMES, HARRIS, and REYNOLD BEAN. *How to Raise Children's Self-Esteem.* Sunnyvale, CA: Enrich Div., 1978.

_____. *How to Teach Children Responsibility.* Sunnyvale, CA: Enrich Div., 1978.

ELKINS, DOV. *Glad to Be Me: Building Self-Esteem in Yourself and Others.* Englewood Cliffs, NJ: Prentice-Hall, Inc., 1976.

_____. *Self Concept Sourcebook.* Rochester, NY: Growth Associates, 1979.

_____. *Teaching People to Love Themselves,* rev. ed. Rochester, NY: Growth Associates, 1978.

FETTIG, ART. *The Three Robots.* Battle Creek, MI: Growth Unlimited, 1981.

FERGUSON, MARILYN. *The Aquarian Conspiracy.* Los Angeles, CA: J. P. Tarcher, Inc., 1980.

GINOTT, HAIM. *Between Teacher and Child.* New York, NY: Macmillan Co., 1972.

GORDON, THOMAS. *Teacher Effectiveness Training.* New York, NY: Peter H. Wyden, 1975.

HENDRICKS, GAY. *The Centering Book: Awareness Activities for Children, Parents, and Teachers.* Englewood Cliffs, NJ: Prentice-Hall, Inc., 1975.

HILL, NAPOLEON, and W. CLEMENT STONE. *Success through a Positive Mental Attitude.* New York, NY: Pocket Books, 1977.

JOHNSON, DAVID. *Reaching Out: Interpersonal Effectiveness and Self-Actualization,* 2nd ed. Englewood Cliffs, NY: Prentice-Hall, Inc., 1981.

_____, and F.P. JOHNSON. *Joining Together: Group Theory and Group Skills,* 2nd ed. Englewood Cliffs, NJ: Prentice-Hall, Inc. 1982.

_____, and ROGER T. JOHNSON. *Learning Together and Alone: Cooperation, Competition, and Individualization.* Englewood Cliffs, NJ: Prentice-Hall, Inc., 1975.

MARTIN, ROBERT J. *Teaching through Encouragement: Techniques to Help Students Learn.* Englewood Cliffs, NJ: Prentice-Hall, Inc., 1980.

MURPHY, JOSEPH. *The Power of Your Subconscious Mind.* Englewood Cliffs, NJ: Prentice-Hall, Inc., 1963.

OSTRANDER, SHEILA, and LYNN SCHROEDER. *Super-Learning.* New York, NY: Delacorte Press and the Confucian Press, Inc., 1980.

PURKEY, WILLIAM WATSON. *Inviting School Success: A Self-Concept Approach to Teaching and Learning.* Belmont, CA: Wadsworth Publishing Co., 1978.

ROY, PATRICIA A., ed. *Structuring Cooperative Learning: The 1982 Handbook.* Minneapolis, MN: Cooperative Network Publications, 1982.

SAMUELS, MIKE, and NANCY SAMUELS. *Seeing with the Mind's Eye: The History, Techniques and Uses of Visualization.* New York, NY: Random House Publishing, 1975.

SAX, SAVILLE, and MERRILL HARMIN. *A Peaceable Classroom: Activities to Calm and Free Student Energies.* Minneapolis, MN: Winston Press, 1977.

SHINN, FLORENCE SCOVEL. *The Game of Life and How to Play It.* Marina Del Rey, CA: DeVorss and Company, 1925.

SIMON, SIDNEY R. *I Am Loveable and Capable.* Allen, TX: Argus Communications, 1973.

_____. *Vulture.* Allen, TX: Argus Communications, 1977.

SMITH, ARDEN. *Giving Kids a Piece of the Action.* Doylestown, PA: TACT, 1977.

STANFORD, GENE. *Developing Effective Classroom Groups.* New York, NY: Hart Publishing Co., 1977.

STOCKING, S. HOLLY, DIANA AREZZO, and SHELLEY LEAVITT. *Helping Kids Make Friends.* Allen, TX: Argus Communications, 1979.

TIMMERMANN, TIM, and DIANE BLECHA. *Modern Stress: The Needless Killer.* Dubuque, IA: Kendall Hunt Publishing Company, 1982.

TRAINING AND WORKSHOPS

Professional training on the concepts presented in this book is available through the Institute for Personal Power, P.O. Box 68, Portage, Michigan 49081 (616) 327-2761.

Two-Hour Awareness Session: This session is designed to give participants an increased awareness of the "Our Classroom" concept. It is an overview of the "Our Classroom" training and gives participants an understanding of what the full training involves. The awareness session is intended for teachers and administrators who are considering receiving further training.

One-Day Awareness Session: The one-day program is designed for teachers and administrators who desire more than a general awareness of "Our Classroom" concepts, and do not choose the full four-day training. Strategies from each of the three modules--Belonging, Classroom Management, and Human-ness--are presented.

Four-Day Skill Training: This training is skill oriented, in-depth and gives participants the greatest understanding of "Our Classroom" ideas and strategies. Participants actively experience many of the ideas and concepts being presented.

The four-day training option helps teachers to:

- create a preventive atmosphere, where discipline problems are less likely to occur;
- provide ways that students can experience responsibility and help them grow in the use of that responsibility;
- develop vehicles for increasing student input, fostering the notion that "I have a stake in this environment;"
- explore specific behaviors that give students room to initiate, discover, and assume individual degrees of control over their own school lives;
- create a classroom atmosphere that develops tradition by helping students experience a sense of rootedness;
- share control by learning appropriate ways to make themselves dispensible.

Other Training Options: "Our Classroom" training can be adjusted to fit time frames other than the one or four-day session. Training can be expanded or compressed to fit the specific needs and resources of your school district.

OTHER TRAINING FROM THE INSTITUTE FOR PERSONAL POWER:

- Cooperative Learning
- Developing Positive Attitudes in Students
- Conducting more Effective Parent-Teacher Conferences
- Supervising Through Social Styles
- The Four Conditions of Self-Esteem

For information on these or other trainings offered by the Institute for Personal Power write:

Institute for Personal Power
P.O. Box 68
Portage, MI 49081
(616) 327-2761
Soft cover $9.95 (add 10% postage)

OTHER BOOKS AND TAPES OFFERED THROUGH
THE INSTITUTE FOR PERSONAL POWER

A GUIDEBOOK FOR COOPERATIVE LEARNING: A TECHNIQUE FOR CREATING MORE EFFECTIVE SCHOOLS
by Dee Dishon and Patricia Wilson O'Leary
paperback ($19.00 pre-paid; $21.00 purchase order)

This guidebook helps classroom teachers enhance their students' achievement through the implementation of cooperative learning activities. Research shows that cooperative methods of instruction and learning develop peer support, provide high motivation, increase on-task time, elicit higher achievement, foster positive attitudes, and facilitate a desirable school climate. The procedures outlined in this book are appropriate for all levels and content areas--from preschool through graduate school. This guidebook helps educators teach students how to work productively and enjoyably in groups while achieving academic goals. Students who work in classrooms where cooperative groups are used learn to care about others. They learn not only to tolerate individual differences, but to value them as well. Acquisition of the important social skills which are learned in cooperative groups has far-reaching implications beyond the classroom to the school, home and community as students carry these skills into their daily lives.

STRATEGIES FOR WINNING TEACHING
with Chick Moorman

Two cassette tapes and binder

$15.95/tapes and binder (add 10% postage)

This cassette-tape program delivers practical, proven strategies for winning teaching. Packed with energy, motivation and power, this 75-minute program is a lesson in the power of belief. You can use it to:

- become more powerful and experience more enjoyment of your professional practice,
- help students learn to believe in themselves,
- re-vitalize, re-energize, and re-inspire yourself, your students, or your staff

Learn to get the Force working with you by:

- employing the doughnut theory and always expecting the best
- sharing yourself with students
- concentrating on "I Can-ness"
- becoming solution-oriented
- activating the success cycle for you and your students

TALK SENSE TO YOURSELF: *The Language of Personal Power*
by Chick Moorman

Soft cover $9.95 (add 10% postage)

There is a connection between the words you use, the beliefs you hold, and the actions you take. This book explores that connection and shows you how you can purposefully select language that creates within you the programming necessary to change the quality and direction of your life.

Contained within this book is a series of words, phrases and ways of speaking that will increase your sense of personal power.

TALK SENSE TO YOURSELF: The Language of Personal Power will help you structure your language patterns to put more choice and possibility in your life. You will become more self-confident, improve your self-esteem, and learn how to talk sense to yourself.

All of the materials described in this section may be ordered through The Institute for Personal Power, P.O. Box 68, Portage, MI, 49801 (616) 327-2761.

index